MADELEINE ALBRIGHT

WOMEN of ACHIEVEMENT

MADELEINE ALBRIGHT

Judy L. Hasday, Ed.M.

CHELSEA HOUSE PUBLISHERS
PHILADELPHIA

> TO MY MOTHER, *who has always believed in my endless possibilities.*

Frontis: Secretary of State Madeleine Albright gazes toward communist North Korea in February 1997 as a U.S. Army sergeant describes the heavy fortifications in the border village of Panmunjom.

Chelsea House Publishers
EDITOR IN CHIEF Stephen Reginald
PRODUCTION MANAGER Pamela Loos
PICTURE EDITOR Judy L. Hasday
ART DIRECTOR Sara Davis
MANAGING EDITOR James D. Gallagher
SENIOR PRODUCTION EDITOR Lisa Chippendale

Staff for **Madeleine Albright**
SENIOR EDITOR Therese De Angelis
ASSOCIATE ART DIRECTOR Takeshi Takahashi
DESIGNER Keith Trego
PICTURE RESEARCHER Patricia Burns
COVER ILLUSTRATION Jim Campbell

The Chelsea House World Wide Website address is
http://www.chelseahouse.com

3 5 7 9 8 6 4 2

Library of Congress Cataloging-in-Publication Data

Hasday, Judy L., 1957-
Madeleine Albright / by Judy L. Hasday.
136 pp.   cm. — (Women of achievement)
Includes bibliographical references and index.
Summary: Focuses on the accomplishments of the former United States ambassador to the United Nations who became the first woman to serve as Secretary of State.

ISBN 0-7910-4708-3. — ISBN 0-7910-4709-1 (pbk.)

1. Albright, Madeleine Korbel—Juvenile literature. 2. Women cabinet officers—United States —Biography—juvenile literature. 3. Cabinet officers—United States—Biography—Juvenile literature. 4. United Nations—Officials and employees—Biography—Juvenile literature. 5. Ambassadors—United States—Biography—Juvenile literature. [1. Albright, Madeleine Korbel. 2. Cabinet officers. 3. Ambassadors. 4. Women—Biography.] I. Title. II. Series.
E840.8.A37H37 1998
327.73'0092—dc21   98-14110
[b]   CIP
                                                    AC

CONTENTS

WOMEN of ACHIEVEMENT

Abigail Adams
WOMEN'S RIGHTS ADVOCATE

Jane Addams
SOCIAL WORKER

Madeleine Albright
STATESWOMAN

Louisa May Alcott
AUTHOR

Marian Anderson
SINGER

Susan B. Anthony
WOMAN SUFFRAGIST

Ethel Barrymore
ACTRESS

Clara Barton
AMERICAN RED CROSS FOUNDER

Elizabeth Blackwell
PHYSICIAN

Margaret Bourke–White
PHOTOGRAPHER

Pearl Buck
AUTHOR

Rachel Carson
BIOLOGIST AND AUTHOR

Mary Cassatt
ARTIST

Hillary Rodham Clinton
FIRST LADY/ATTORNEY

Agnes de Mille
CHOREOGRAPHER

Diana, Princess of Wales
HUMANITARIAN

Emily Dickinson
POET

Elizabeth Dole
POLITICIAN

Isadora Duncan
DANCER

Amelia Earhart
AVIATOR

Jodie Foster
ACTRESS/DIRECTOR

Betty Friedan
FEMINIST

Althea Gibson
TENNIS CHAMPION

Ruth Bader Ginsburg
SUPREME COURT JUSTICE

Helen Hayes
ACTRESS

Katharine Hepburn
ACTRESS

Anne Hutchinson
RELIGIOUS LEADER

Mahalia Jackson
GOSPEL SINGER

Helen Keller
HUMANITARIAN

Jeane Kirkpatrick
DIPLOMAT

Barbara McClintock
BIOLOGIST

Margaret Mead
ANTHROPOLOGIST

Edna St. Vincent Millay
POET

Julia Morgan
ARCHITECT

Grandma Moses
PAINTER

Lucretia Mott
WOMAN SUFFRAGIST

Sandra Day O'Connor
SUPREME COURT JUSTICE

Rosie O'Donnell
ENTERTAINER/COMEDIAN

Georgia O'Keeffe
PAINTER

Eleanor Roosevelt
DIPLOMAT AND HUMANITARIAN

Wilma Rudolph
CHAMPION ATHLETE

Elizabeth Cady Stanton
WOMAN SUFFRAGIST

Gloria Steinem
FEMINIST

Harriet Beecher Stowe
AUTHOR AND ABOLITIONIST

Barbra Streisand
ENTERTAINER

Elizabeth Taylor
ACTRESS/ACTIVIST

**Abigail Van Buren/
Ann Landers**
COLUMNISTS

Barbara Walters
JOURNALIST

Edith Wharton
AUTHOR

Phyllis Wheatley
POET

Babe Didrikson Zaharias
CHAMPION ATHLETE

"REMEMBER THE LADIES"

MATINA S. HORNER

"Remember the Ladies." That is what Abigail Adams wrote to her husband John, then a delegate to the Continental Congress, as the Founding Fathers met in Philadelphia to form a new nation in March of 1776. "Be more generous and favorable to them than your ancestors. Do not put such limited power in the hands of the Husbands. If particular care and attention is not paid to the Ladies," Abigail Adams warned, "we are determined to foment a Rebellion, and will not hold ourselves bound by any Laws in which we have no voice, or Representation."

The words of Abigail Adams, one of the earliest American advocates of women's rights, were prophetic. Because when we have not "remembered the ladies," they have, by their words and deeds, reminded us so forcefully of the omission that we cannot fail to remember them. For the history of American women is as interesting and varied as the history of our nation as a whole. American women have played an integral part in founding, settling, and building our country. Some we remember as remarkable women who—against great odds—achieved distinction in the public arena: Anne Hutchinson, who in the 17th century became a charismatic religious leader; Phillis Wheatley, an 18th-century black slave who became a poet; Susan B. Anthony, whose name is synonymous with the 19th-century women's rights movement, and who led the struggle to enfranchise women; and in the 20th century, Amelia Earhart, the first woman to cross the Atlantic Ocean by air.

These extraordinary women certainly merit our admiration, but other women, "common women," many of them all but forgotten, should also be recognized for their contributions to American thought and culture. Women have been community builders; they have founded schools and formed voluntary associations to help those in need; they have assumed the major responsibility for rearing children, passing on from one generation to the next the values that keep a culture alive. These and innumerable other contributions, once ignored, are now being recognized by scholars, students, and the public. It is exciting and gratifying that a part of our history that was hardly acknowledged a few generations ago is now being studied and brought to light.

In recent decades, the field of women's history has grown from obscurity to a politically controversial splinter movement to academic respectability, in many cases mainstreamed into such traditional disciplines as history, economics, and psychology. Scholars of women, both female and male, have organized research centers at such prestigious institutions as Wellesley College, Stanford University, and the University of California. Other notable centers for women's studies are the Center for the American Woman and Politics at the Eagleton Institute of Politics at Rutgers University; the Henry A. Murray Research Center for the Study of Lives, at Radcliffe College; and the Women's Research and Education Institute, the research arm of the Congressional Caucus on Women's Issues. Other scholars and public figures have established archives and libraries, such as the Schlesinger Library on the History of Women in America, at Radcliffe College, and the Sophia Smith Collection, at Smith College, to collect and preserve the written and tangible legacies of women.

From the initial donation of the Women's Rights Collection in 1943, the Schlesinger Library grew to encompass vast collections documenting the manifold accomplishments of American women. Simultaneously, the women's movement in general and the academic discipline of women's studies in particular also began with a narrow definition and gradually expanded their mandate. Early causes, such as woman suffrage and social reform, abolition, and organized labor were joined by newer concerns, such as the history of women in business and the professions and in politics and government; the study of the family; and social issues such as health policy and education.

Women, as historian Arthur M. Schlesinger, jr., once pointed out, "have constituted the most spectacular casualty of traditional history. They have made up at least half the human race, but you could never tell that by looking at the books historians write." The new breed of historians is remedying that omission. They have written books about immigrant women and about working-class women who struggled for survival in cities and about black women who met the challenges of life in rural areas. They are telling the stories of women who, despite the barriers of tradition and economics, became lawyers and doctors and public figures.

The women's studies movement has also led scholars to question traditional interpretations of their respective disciplines. For example, the study of war has traditionally been an exercise in military and political analysis, an examination of strategies planned and executed by men. But scholars of women's history have pointed out that wars have also been periods of tremendous change and even opportunity for women, because the very absence of men on the home front enabled them to expand their educational, economic, and professional activities and to assume leadership in their homes.

The early scholars of women's history showed a unique brand of courage in choosing to investigate new subjects and take new approaches to old ones. Often, like their subjects, they endured criticism and even ostracism by their academic colleagues. But their efforts have unquestionably been worthwhile, because with the publication of each new study and book another piece of the historical patchwork is sewn into place, revealing an increasingly comprehensive picture of the role of women in our rich and varied history.

Such books on groups of women are essential, but books that focus on the lives of individuals are equally indispensable. Biographies can be inspirational, offering their readers the example of people with vision who have looked outside themselves for their goals and have often struggled against great obstacles to achieve them. Marian Anderson, for instance, had to overcome racial bigotry in order to perfect her art and perform as a concert singer. Isadora Duncan defied the rules of classical dance to find true artistic freedom. Jane Addams had to break down society's notions of the proper role for women in order to create new social situations, notably the settlement house. All of these women had to come to terms both with themselves and with the world in which they lived. Only then could they move ahead as pioneers in their chosen callings.

Biography can inspire not only by adulation but also by realism. It helps us to see not only the qualities in others that we hope to emulate, but also, perhaps, the weaknesses that made them "human." By helping us identify with the subject on a more personal level they help us feel that we, too, can achieve such goals. We read about Eleanor Roosevelt, for instance, who occupied a unique and seemingly enviable position as the wife of the president. Yet we can sympathize with her inner dilemma; an inherently shy woman, she had to force herself to live a most public life in order to use her position to benefit others. We may not be able to imagine ourselves having the immense poetic talent of Emily Dickinson, but from her story we can understand the challenges faced by a creative woman who was expected to fulfill many family responsibilities. And though few of us will ever reach the level of athletic accomplishment displayed by Wilma Rudolph or Babe Zaharias, we can still appreciate their spirit, their overwhelming will to excel.

A biography is a multifaceted lens. It is first of all a magnification, the intimate examination of one particular life. But at the same time, it is a wide-angle lens, informing us about the world in which the subject lived. We come away from reading about one life knowing more about the social, political, and economic fabric of the time. It is for this reason, perhaps, that the great New England essayist Ralph Waldo Emerson wrote in 1841, "There is properly no history: only biography." And it is also why biography, and particularly women's biography, will continue to fascinate writers and readers alike.

The crowning achievement in a remarkable career: Madeleine Albright's three daughters and President Bill Clinton look on as Vice President Al Gore swears in Albright, the first female secretary of state, on January 23, 1997.

1

YOUR NEW ADDRESS, MS. ALBRIGHT: FOGGY BOTTOM

"**S**he watched her world fall apart, and ever since, she has dedicated her life to spreading to the rest of the world the freedom and tolerance her family found here in America." These were the words of President Bill Clinton on December 5, 1996, when he introduced Madeleine Korbel Albright as the new U.S. secretary of state. Albright's nomination had been confirmed by the U.S. Senate in a unanimous vote of 99-0. (Only West Virginia senator Jay Rockefeller did not vote; however, he later expressed his support of Albright's confirmation.) The historical significance of the event attracted worldwide media attention: in the more than 200 years since America was founded, no woman had ever been appointed secretary of state, the fourth-highest-ranking government position in the country.

But Albright herself had long since made her mark in the world of foreign relations. Nearly four years earlier, in January 1993, Clinton had named her the United States permanent representative to the United Nations (a position commonly referred to as U.S. ambassador to the U.N.). Even then, she was not low-key in her approach to foreign diplomacy. While at the U.N., Albright strongly lobbied for the use of American military force in the eastern European country of Bosnia, where a civil war raged out of control. "What's the point of having this superb military you're always talking about if we can't use it?" Albright declared to Colin Powell, who was chairman of the Joint Chiefs of Staff. And in July 1994, she delivered a blunt summary of America's military and political resolve to the illegal martial government of Haiti: "You can depart voluntarily and soon," she told its members, "or you can depart involuntarily and soon."

Madeleine Albright assumed the duties of secretary of state after Warren Christopher, who served during Clinton's first four years as president, announced his retirement. Christopher had logged over 723,000 miles shuttling around the globe, most frequently to the political hotbed of the Middle East, and was known for his genteel diplomatic demeanor. Albright, by contrast, is known for speaking much more directly, and she approaches foreign relations diplomacy in an entirely different way. On her first day as secretary of state, she met with her staff and set the tone immediately: "I have to warn you I have a way of disregarding the bureaucratic structure and going to people directly. So I apologize in advance." A passionate advocate of democracy and of monitoring human rights issues around the world, Albright has often pressed for U.S. intervention in foreign conflicts, believing that only the United States has the military power and political influence to help resolve such situations swiftly. Because of her aggressive, proactive approach to international strife, Albright has often been labeled a "hawk" (one who advocates the use of military force to carry out foreign policy) by many political analysts and government officials.

As secretary of state, Albright is following in the footsteps of such notable Americans as Thomas Jefferson, a founding father and author of the Declaration of Independence; William H. Seward (appointed in

1861); William Jennings Bryan (1913); George C. Marshall (1947); and Henry Kissinger (1973). Another former secretary of state holds a more personal significance for Albright. Edmund Muskie, who was appointed to the position in 1980, had long been a mentor of Albright's. Albright first became involved in politics while campaigning for Muskie during his 1968 run for the presidency. Eight years later, she became Senator Muskie's chief legislative assistant.

The secretary of state is the top-ranking member of the president's cabinet, which includes the heads of all 14 executive departments of the federal government: Agriculture, Commerce, Defense, Education, Energy, Health and Human Services, Housing and Urban Development, Interior, Justice, Labor, State, Transportation, Treasury, and Veterans Affairs. Other cabinet

Albright first drew worldwide attention as the U.S. ambassador to the United Nations, where she was known for her outspokenness on human rights issues and her strong pro-democracy stance.

officials include the director of the Central Intelligence Agency (CIA), the White House chief of staff, and the counsel to the president. In addition, the Offices of Management and Budget and the U.S. Trade Representative have cabinet rank in the Clinton administration. All cabinet members are appointed by the president; although they are not elected officials, all of the president's appointees must be confirmed by the Senate before they can assume their posts.

Cabinet members are selected by the president for various reasons, including their experience or expertise in a given area or special talents they may have. They can be political allies, longtime friends, or even relatives of the president. And they come from all walks of life: they may be rich or poor, male or female; they may be bankers, soldiers, researchers, or doctors. Each cabinet member is personally responsible for advising the president on matters pertaining to his or her department. The president relies on these advisors to provide him with up-to-date information on a variety of topics and to counsel him on issues such as security, health, and safety. Since they are not members of either house of Congress, cabinet members may only speak officially to these governing bodies when called upon to testify before congressional committees.

The secretary of state is also a member of the National Security Council (NSC), which was created by Congress in 1947 under President Harry S. Truman. The NSC is the president's primary forum for discussing and debating matters of national security and foreign policy with his senior advisors and cabinet members. NSC members advise and assist the president on such matters and execute policy decisions relating to national security.

In addition to the permanent members of the NSC—the president, vice president, secretaries of state and defense, chairman of the Joint Chiefs of Staff, and director of the CIA—other officials are also invited to

attend council meetings. Among those invited is the U.N. ambassador. For this reason, Madeleine Albright was familiar with Clinton's views on foreign policy issues long before her appointment as secretary of state.

The secretary of state is the most important member of the president's cabinet for many reasons. She is fourth in order of succession to the presidency after the vice president, the speaker of the House, and the president *pro tempore* (Latin meaning "for the time being") of the Senate. As President Clinton's principal advisor on foreign policy, Secretary Albright is responsible for directing, supervising, and coordinating U.S. relations and activities around the world.

A large part of the secretary of state's job is to com-

"You can depart voluntarily and soon, or you can depart involuntarily and soon," U.N. Ambassador Albright told the military government of Haiti in 1994. Here Albright (top center) speaks to a throng of reporters outside the presidential palace in Haiti's capital, Port-au-Prince.

Afghan girls in traditional costumes present bouquets to Secretary of State Madeleine Albright during her November 1997 visit to an Afghan refugee camp in Pakistan. "It is not too much to say," Albright declared during an address to her staff, "that upon successful American diplomacy depends the future of the world."

municate U.S. foreign policy to other countries. Madeleine Albright accomplishes this by traveling widely and frequently to meet with prime ministers, monarchs, and other heads of state. Many of these visits have defined purposes, such as negotiating treaties or trade agreements. Other visits are scheduled simply to stay in contact with foreign officials. By maintaining diplomatic representation abroad, the secretary of state promotes good international relations for the United States.

The State Department is also recognized as the symbolic guardian of the nation's security—it is the keeper of the Great Seal of the United States. The seal, which was adopted on June 20, 1782, represented the creation of a new nation of equal importance to other nations of the world, many of which had their own seals of sovereignty. Today, the Great Seal is used only to certify presidential proclamations, treaties, and other official documents. A representation of the Great Seal can be found on the back of the American one-dollar bill.

It is vital that the secretary of state remain on good terms not only with foreign dignitaries but also with politicians in her own country—the members of the House of Representatives and the Senate, the two governing bodies of the United States. The Senate must approve all treaties arranged by the secretary, and the House controls the funds that the secretary needs to carry out foreign policy. Madeleine Albright has become adept at cultivating alliances with the most important and influential members of Congress. Her most unlikely affiliation has been with conservative Republican senator Jesse Helms, the irascible chairman of the Senate Foreign Relations Committee who is known for his outspoken views on decisions affecting U.S. domestic and foreign policy.

The Department of State is the highest-ranking executive agency in the United States government. Originally called the Department of Foreign Affairs, it was established, with the Departments of Treasury and War, when the U.S. Constitution was adopted in 1789. At that time, the State Department's functions included operating the mint, issuing patents for inventions, taking the national census, and supervising territorial affairs while the country was still growing geographically. Most of these responsibilities have since been turned over to other government bureaus or departments.

The first secretary of state was Thomas Jefferson, who was appointed by President George Washington in 1789. Jefferson's responsibilities were somewhat different from those held by modern secretaries of state. In the late 18th and early 19th centuries, the post was often considered a stepping-stone to the presidency. Jefferson, James Madison, James Monroe, John Quincy Adams, Martin Van Buren, and James Buchanan were all elected president after serving in the State Department. (Because Madeleine Albright is not a natural citi-

Responding to remarks that he had chosen Albright solely because of her gender, President Clinton said, "She got the job because I believe . . . she had the best combination of qualities to succeed and to serve our country at this moment in history."

zen of the United States—that is, she was not born in this country—she is not eligible to become president.)

By the 1900s, secretaries were selected primarily for their experience in foreign affairs. For example, Cordell Hull, a Nobel Peace Prize–winner, served in both the Senate and the House prior to his appointment as secretary of state in 1933. And John Foster Dulles, who was named to the position in 1953, had been a U.N. delegate and a senator before his appointment.

Today, the offices of Secretary of State Albright and those of her top aides are located on the seventh floor of 2201 C Street N.W., in the Foggy Bottom section of Washington, D.C. Although the organization and composition of the U.S. Department of State have changed, its primary objectives have not. Albright's aides assist her with special projects such as treaty negotiations, but the department's main responsibility is to carry out American foreign policy according to the president's direction.

The State Department also continuously monitors the international activities of its allies and adversaries. It accomplishes this through its overseas missions called embassies, which handle issues between governments. Other missions, known as consulates, handle such matters as issuing visas to foreign citizens to enter the United States and passports to American citizens who wish to travel abroad.

For Madeleine Albright, the journey to her confirmation as the 64th secretary of state spanned two continents and 20 years of government service. She earned a master's degree and a Ph.D. in public law and government from Columbia University in New York City. She served as professor of foreign policy at Georgetown University in Washington, D.C., before she was appointed American ambassador to the U.N. It was as though Albright had been preparing to take her place in American history for most of her life. As President Clinton remarked during Secretary Albright's swearing-in on January 23, 1997:

> Arriving on our shores as a refugee from tyranny and oppression, she worked her way up with determination and character to attain our nation's highest diplomatic office. She knows from her life's experience that freedom has its price and democracy its rewards. Her story is the best of America's story, told with courage, compassion, and conviction.

Madeleine Albright's story begins far from the political spotlight of Washington. Before becoming secretary of state, the one-time refugee from Czechoslovakia would have great distances to travel, not only geographically but also politically and personally. Her appetite for political knowledge and her passion for freedom and democracy are the vehicles that carried her on that journey.

Tomáš Masaryk (center, near the crack on the bell) and other representatives of Central European countries gather around the Liberty Bell in Philadelphia, Pennsylvania, on October 26, 1918. The previous month, the United States had officially acknowledged the National Council of the Czech Lands as a legitimate and independent government.

2

A HOMELAND IS BORN

Even as a child, Madeleine Albright was no stranger to politics. Her father, Josef, was a diplomat with the Czechoslovakian government before the outbreak of World War II and served during the war with the exiled Czech government in London, England.

Born in Prague, Czechoslovakia, on May 15, 1937, Marie Jana Korbel (later nicknamed Madeleine by her grandmother) was the first child of Mandula and Josef Korbel. Her father's family origins can be traced back to the small Moravian town of Kysperk (now known as Letohrad). There, her grandfather Arnost Korbel co-managed a match factory with a man named Jan Reinelt. Arnost was well liked in the community and was considered generous and dynamic by neighbors, employees, and business associates.

Arnost and his wife, Olga, had three children, a daughter and two sons. Margareta, the oldest, eventually married a local doctor. Jan followed in his father's footsteps by going into the family business. The youngest child, Josef, Madeleine's father, chose to pursue a career in government.

Born in 1909, Josef lived with his family in a region that for hundreds of years had been under the rule of the Hapsburg

Arnost Korbel (center) in a formal portrait with his sons, Josef (left) and Jan (right). The senior Korbel is still remembered by people in his hometown of Letohrad as a warm and generous man.

Empire. The Holy Roman Empire, founded in 962 A.D. when Otto I was made emperor, included the regions of modern-day Austria, Switzerland, Bohemia, and part of France and Italy, as well as the kingdom of Germany. From 1273 to 1806, the Holy Roman Empire was ruled by the Hapsburgs, a German royal family. Although French leader Napoléon Bonaparte abolished the empire in 1806, the Hapsburgs continued to govern the Austrian Empire, which included Bohemia and Moravia. In 1867, the Hapsburgs extended their reign beyond Austria and Hungary, eventually annexing the provinces of Bosnia and Herzegovina.

The new Austro-Hungarian sovereignty was comprised of many different peoples and cultures. It was made up of more than 23 million Slavs (including Czechs and Serbs), 12 million Germans, 10 million Magyars, 3 million Romanians, and scores of smaller ethnic groups who had settled in this European region.

These peoples retained their own cultures, referring to themselves by their own nationalities and continuing to speak their native languages and practice their own customs. Most of the peoples under this joint sovereignty were far more interested in establishing their own independence than in working for the betterment of the ruling monarchy. During the remainder of the 19th century, widespread discontent simmered throughout Austria-Hungary. Under this feudal-like system of government, the aristocracy—the Germans—enjoyed prosperous and privileged lives, while the Czechs, Slovaks, and other peoples mostly struggled in poverty.

Madeleine's father grew up like most children of small central European towns during that period. He played marbles and hide-and-seek with his friends and went to the local school. However, he wasn't growing up in a country united by common ideals and a common language like his counterparts in America. Nor were his people free to practice self-government.

While Josef was still a child, a young Czech patriot named Tomáš Masaryk was dreaming of a time when Czechs and Slovaks would be free from the oppressive Hapsburgs and would unite to form a single independent state. In his book *Tomáš Masaryk*, author Gavin Lewis described Masaryk's aim:

> As a child [Masaryk] learned to hate Austria-Hungary's rigidly authoritarian society and its ruling dynasty, the Hapsburgs. As a professor of philosophy at the Czech University of Prague, Masaryk carried on a relentless pursuit of the truth, winning the support and admiration of some of his students but alienating his colleagues and fellow countrymen by shattering many of their illusions. As a politician, Masaryk advocated the seemingly unrealistic idea of a democratic partnership between the Czechs and their Slovak neighbors.

Tomáš Masaryk's quest to create a free and democratic country would have a profound impact on Josef

Korbel's life and on the lives of millions of other Czechs and Slovaks in the Hapsburg Empire.

During this period, many ethnic cultures across Europe were trying to establish themselves as separate entities by increasing their own wealth and power bases. The provincial city of Prague was one of the many cities affected by this trend, which was known as nationalism. The Czechs called their movement the National Awakening, but for them it was more like a revival than a new concept. Centuries earlier, Bohemia, Moravia, and Silesia had formed an independent kingdom that thrived and prospered until it was taken over by the Hapsburgs. Now the National Awakening looked to revive that spirit of independence. It was gaining momentum, and Masaryk wanted to be a part of it. He would soon have his chance.

When Josef Korbel was just five years old, Archduke Franz Ferdinand, the crown prince of Austria-Hungary, and his wife, Sophie, were assassinated. Convinced that Serbia was behind the assassination plot, Austria-Hungary declared war on its smaller southern neighbor on June 28th, 1914. By that fall, Austria-Hungary, Germany, and Turkey (the Central Powers) had engaged Belgium, France, Great Britain, Italy, Russia, and Serbia (the Allies) in a full-scale war.

As battles raged across Europe, Tomáš Masaryk went into exile in the politically neutral country of Switzerland. Masaryk had decided when the war broke out that this would be his best chance to seek the help of other countries in winning independence for the Czechs and Slovaks. First, he had to convince the leaders of the Allied countries that overthrowing the Hapsburgs and granting independence to Czechoslovakia was in their best interests. Over the next two years, Masaryk and two colleagues, Eduard Beneš and Milan Stefanik, rallied support for their cause. In 1916, they formed an organization called the National Council of the Czech Lands, which Beneš operated from an office in Paris, France. At

the same time, Stefanik appealed to the roughly 100,000 Czechs in Russia, while Masaryk sought the aid of Czech and Slovak emigrants to the United States. Masaryk also assembled an army of Czechs 40,000 strong, called the Czechoslovak Legion, to fight on the side of the Allies. The Legion demonstrated, said Masaryk, "that we value our freedom higher than our lives."

In 1917 the United States joined the Allies. The following year, on May 4, Masaryk arrived in Chicago, Illinois, home to the second-largest Czech community in the world, to drum up support for the Czech cause. He then traveled to Washington, D.C., taking his cam-

American soldiers and tanks advance through the Forest of Argonne, France, in the fall of 1918. The infusion of fresh U.S. troops in 1917 allowed the Allied forces to gain the upper hand in World War I, which ended just two months after this photograph was taken.

Tomáš Masaryk (front row, center, in white hat) and the members of the Czechoslovak Legion, who fought for independence during World War I.

paign directly to President Woodrow Wilson. He told Wilson that the "Czechoslovak fight against the Hapsburgs was just like the American struggle against George III [during the American Revolutionary War] and that the future Czechoslovakia would be a government of the people, by the people, and for the people, just like the United States." Masaryk eventually won President Wilson's support. On September 3, 1918, America acknowledged the National Council of the Czech Lands as a legitimate government. The United States also affirmed that, in joining the Allies, the Czechs and Slovaks were struggling for their own independence as well.

America's entry into the war bolstered the strength of

the Allied Forces, and finally the Central Powers wore down. It was obvious by the autumn of 1918 that the Central Powers would be defeated. One by one, beginning with Bulgaria and Turkey, members began signing peace treaties with the Allies. The Czechs, Slovaks, Hungarians, and Poles declared their independence, and the Austro-Hungarian Empire collapsed. Former emperor Charles I signed a treaty on November 3, 1918; Germany followed suit a week later. The Allied forces had won the war.

The losses suffered in World War I were tremendous. More than 8.5 million soldiers and as many as 12.5 million civilians had died in the four years of battles that ravaged most of Europe. More than $125 billion were spent by the Allies; more than $186 billion were spent by the Central Powers. But human casualties and economic losses were only part of the picture. The political changes wrought by the war radically altered the face of Europe. New countries emerged, and existing countries acquired or lost territory. Where the Austro-Hungarian Empire had existed, there were now the countries of Czechoslovakia, Romania, Yugoslavia, the Austrian Republic, and Hungary.

Although all fighting had ceased by the end of 1918, the war was not officially over until the signing of the Treaty of Versailles, which took place on June 28, 1919. Thirty-two allied nations participated in negotiating the treaty; though the United States helped draft the document, it never ratified it.

Because of Germany's excessive aggression during the war, the heaviest penalties were levied against that country. Four major provisions were set forth in the treaty. First, Germany was to cede land to France, Poland, Denmark, Belgium, Lithuania, and Czechoslovakia. It also relinquished its colonies, including territory in Africa. Second, it was ordered to pay $33 billion in reparations to the Allies. Third, Germany's military force was reduced to 100,000 soldiers. The fourth and

Georges Clemenceau, head of the French delegation, stands to address representatives from 32 nations gathered in the Hall of Mirrors in Versailles, France. To his right is U.S. president Woodrow Wilson. The Treaty of Versailles was the result of months of bitter negotiating known as the Paris Peace Conference. Among its provisions was the creation of the League of Nations, a precursor of the United Nations.

final provision created the League of Nations, the first international organization of countries instituted to ensure the collective security of the world against the emergence of future aggressors. The League aimed to accomplish this goal by arbitrating disputes between countries, monitoring weapons manufacturing and testing, and exercising a policy of open diplomacy with all its members and nonmembers. The League was basically created to function as a world court of law.

For the countries who fought alongside the Allies, the end of the war brought hope and relief. Only a few months earlier, Prague and other cities and towns within the Austro-Hungarian Empire had been on the losing side. Now they had cause to rejoice. To the millions of Czechs and Slovaks who waited for a time when they would be free and self-governing, the formation of an independent Czechoslovakia was a dream come true. And the man who had done much to realize that dream—Tomáš Masaryk—became Czechoslovakia's first president. His colleague Eduard Beneš was appointed his minister of foreign affairs.

December 21, 1918, the day of Masaryk's return to Czechoslovakia, was a national day of celebration. Schools, factories, and businesses were closed throughout the new sovereignty of Czechoslovakia. Flags of the Allied nations draped city buildings. Children, peasants, and soldiers strolled merrily through the crowded streets. Hordes of Czech and Slovak people gathered in the country's new capital city, Prague, to welcome their new president. No doubt the Korbel family was among the celebrants. At age 9, Josef Korbel was living in a free country for the first time. This taste of freedom forever changed him: he would never again live under the darkness of oppression.

Although the end of the war brought great hope and independence to many in Europe, the League of Nations never really took hold in the postwar period. Germany eventually refused to accept the penalties imposed upon it, and the cost of reparations nearly brought about a complete economic collapse. Its people were ravaged by widespread poverty. Unemployment skyrocketed. Many Germans were starving, and all were desperate for an end to their suffering, which they blamed on the Allies and the League of Nations. This resentment festered for the next 15 years, until a leader emerged who promised to relieve them of their misery. His name was Adolf Hitler.

Czech citizens salute invading German troops with fear and sorrow in Eger, Czechoslovakia. Only 12 days earlier, on September 30, 1938, the Munich Pact had delivered the Czech territory of the Sudetenland into the hands of Adolf Hitler.

3

DARK CLOUDS
OVER EUROPE

After 1918, the countries that had won their independence in World War I began the process of formulating constitutions, electing their own officials, and setting up new governments. While Madeleine Albright's father was still a child, the country he and his family would one day call their homeland was being shaped. Gaining independence had been an intense struggle, but it was only the beginning of the battle to get the new country on its feet.

One of the greatest challenges facing Tomáš Masaryk was finding a way to unite the Czech and Slovak peoples, each group with its own strengths and resources, into one growing and prosperous nation. Though Czechoslovakia was small geographically (about the size of the American state of Alabama), its citizens had much to offer. Many Czechs were well educated and were experienced producers of coal, glass, iron, leather, weapons, and textiles; the Slovaks, though most were peasants and many were illiterate, were nevertheless hardworking people living in a region abundant in raw materials such as timber and minerals.

The shifting political borders of postwar Europe meant that

some Germans and Hungarians also found themselves living in Czechoslovakia. These groups for the most part resented being a part of the population of the new country and made repeated attempts to elicit support for an organized opposition to the government. But the national partnership in Czechoslovakia remained strong in spite of such factions.

In 1928, Arnost and Olga Korbel and their children left Kysperk for the new capital of Prague. Under the leadership of President Masaryk, Czechoslovakia had begun to establish itself as one of the most politically progressive and economically successful countries in Central Europe. Arnost became a large shareholder and company director of a building materials business in Prague, and though he was not a member of the upper class, he was able to provide a comfortable life for his wife and children.

While in Prague, young Josef studied law and in 1933 earned his doctorate. In 1934 he became a diplomat for the Czech foreign service. Josef also had been seeing his high-school sweetheart, Mandula Spieglova, who lived with her parents, Alois and Ruzena, in the neighboring town of Kostelec nad Orlici. In 1935, Josef and Mandula were married.

The newlyweds settled down together during a worldwide economic depression that had begun when the United States stock market collapsed on October 29, 1929. In the crash, hundreds of thousands of people had lost their entire savings. Panic had spread across America and through the rest of the world. Throughout the early 1930s, American banks closed, stores went out of business, farms went into foreclosure, and millions of people lost their jobs. At one point, approximately 25 percent of the working population of America was unemployed, unable to afford food and other daily necessities. Every segment of U.S. society was affected, from doctors and lawyers to merchants, artists, and laborers. Lines formed outside government

soup kitchens as people waited for food handouts.

Though the impact of the Great Depression was felt worldwide, the United States and Germany were hit hardest. Often, civil unrest emerges out of national suffering and hardship, and in Germany this was especially true. Citizens grew impatient when the economy showed no sign of improvement. The country already had been saddled with billions of dollars in reparation costs after World War I; the added impact of this global depression only intensified the restlessness and displeasure that was already spreading through Germany.

The resentment that Germans felt toward the Allied countries who had forged the Treaty of Versailles fed an already heightened sense of nationalism and a desire to purge the country of all those who were not German. At the same time, the anti-Semitic movement that had arisen in Germany during the 19th century was reestab-

An open-air soup kitchen in Berlin, 1918. In part because of the harsh terms imposed on it by the Treaty of Versailles, Germany suffered a severe economic crisis after World War I, marked by widespread unemployment, runaway inflation, and the rise of extremist political parties.

lishing itself. Jews were wrongly held responsible for many of the ills plaguing the country.

In Italy, meanwhile, a dictator named Benito Mussolini had assumed power; in the U.S.S.R. (formerly Russia), the ruthless Joseph Stalin was firmly in control. Likewise, the imperialist government of Japan had embarked on its own military quest to control Asia and the western Pacific. And in Germany, a young, fanatical nationalist, Adolf Hitler, was inspiring his countrymen with his fiery rhetoric.

From his rise to power to his ultimate ruin, Hitler propelled the world into the darkest days of modern history. In his book *Adolf Hitler*, Dennis Wepman describes the dictator's powerful presence and the responsiveness of his countrymen:

> Hitler electrified audiences with his impassioned and theatrical oratory. His speeches—about the supreme importance of loyalty to the "Fatherland" and the injustice of Germany's defeat, which he blamed on the Jews—were received with wild enthusiasm by demoralized, desperate, inflation-ridden Berliners.

Hitler railed against the sanctions imposed upon Germany after the war. His message was simple: the rest of the world was to blame for Germany's current condition, and the causes were easily identifiable. First there was the Treaty of Versailles, which had burdened Germany with intolerable penalties. Hitler was convinced that the Allied forces, jealous and fearful of Germany's superiority as a world power, had tried to decimate the country and humiliate its citizens. Second, he believed that Jews and Communists had been using covert tactics to undermine the true supremacy of Germany. Hitler vowed to restore the country to its former preeminence.

As economic conditions worsened, Hitler and his National Socialist German Workers Party, better known as Nazis, drew even more support. Hitler was defeated

in the 1932 national election by Paul von Hindenburg, who was reelected president. However, in January 1933, Hindenburg appointed Hitler chancellor—the chief executive of the Republic of Germany—believing that by doing so he could more easily control his opponent. For many other ambitious politicians, this successful ascension to power would have been the consummation of a professional career. But for Hitler, it was merely a step closer to his final goal: complete control over Germany and its future and eventually over Europe itself. He did not have to wait long. When Hindenburg died on August 2, 1934, Adolf Hitler immediately assumed the

A chilling alliance: German chancellor Adolf Hitler, second from right, and Italian premier Benito Mussolini, far right, review an Italian honor guard gathered to welcome Hitler to Venice on June 14, 1933.

authority of the president and changed his title to *Führer* (leader), abolishing the presidency.

With complete control of the government and the full support of his party, Hitler began to move more aggressively with his plans for restoring the country to its former cultural, economic, and military greatness. He had been rebuilding the German military in direct defiance of the Treaty of Versailles, but the League of Nations did not take action. An uneasiness began to envelop Europe once more.

While these dark clouds were gathering, Josef and Mandula Korbel were celebrating the birth of their first child, Marie (Madeleine). Josef had received his first foreign assignment as press attaché in the Czech Embassy of Yugoslavia. Upon moving to Belgrade, Yugoslavia's capital, the Korbels found themselves in an environment that was much more rural and less developed than Prague. Nonetheless, Josef, Mandula, and little Madeleine adjusted well to their new home. Jara Ribnikar and her husband, Vlado, were friends of the Korbels' in Yugoslavia. Years later, she remembered them fondly. "Belgrade was like a village in those days," she said. "Everybody knew everybody else. The Korbels's house was always open. [Josef] had a way of encouraging talented people."

In 1936, with virtually no opposition from the League of Nations, Hitler seized the Rhineland, an area west of the Rhine River, where the Allies had forbidden Germany to station troops. That year, he also completed his alliance with Mussolini: the two dictators, with an eye toward controlling all of Europe, created what they called the Rome-Berlin Axis, an imaginary line spanning the continent and connecting the capital cities of Italy and Germany. In 1938, Hitler invaded Austria, thereby successfully completing what he called *Anschluss* (political unification) with Austria—another violation of the Treaty of Versailles.

Hitler next looked to overtake the Sudetenland, an

area of west Czechoslovakia that the Treaty of Versailles had taken from Germany. The Sudetenland was not only rich in natural resources but was also home to more than three million German people. Although Czechoslovakia had made a number of concessions to the Sudeten Germans, they were not enough for Hitler. He justified his actions by asserting that the Sudeten Germans were suffering at the hands of Czech oppressors because of their "sympathy and unity" with Nazism.

In Czechoslovakia, meanwhile, Eduard Beneš had succeeded Tomáš Masaryk as president in 1935. Masaryk died in the fall of 1937 and was thus spared the pain of seeing his life's work crushed by the seemingly boundless voracity of Adolf Hitler. Though most countries by now recognized that Germany was on the march again, none of them wanted to risk a direct confrontation with Hitler. On September 30, 1938, Great Britain and France, in an attempt to end diplomatical-

Mandula and Josef Korbel during the early years of their marriage. Madeleine Albright has described her parents as "passionate about Czechoslovakia and dedicated to doing what they could to improve things. They instilled that in me."

ly this latest threat to peace in Europe, reached an agreement with Germany and Italy known as the Munich Pact. Signed by Hitler, British prime minister Neville Chamberlain, French premier Edouard Daladier, and Mussolini, the pact allowed Germany to take over the Sudetenland, provided it made no further territorial demands.

Although Beneš had been willing to resist Hitler's demands, his Western European allies insisted on this concession. Beneš and his cabinet members resigned from their positions immediately. Chamberlain later hailed the Munich Pact for bringing "peace in our time."

A few months after the pact was reached, Josef Korbel was ordered to return to Prague from his post in Belgrade. He spent the next few months working at the Czech ministry's headquarters. Now Germany was pressuring Czechoslovakia to grant self-rule to several Czech and Slovak provinces within its borders. The threat of a full-scale German invasion loomed.

Europe now knew that Hitler could not be trusted or controlled. Even France and Great Britain had begun fortifying their own borders and beefing up their armed forces against a possible German invasion. In the early morning hours of March 15, 1939, under the pretense of restoring German-speaking areas to Germany, Hitler's tanks rolled into Prague and took over Czechoslovakia.

In his memoir, *From Prague After Munich*, George F. Kennan, at the time a member of the United States legation in Prague, describes the scene on that disastrous day:

> A full blizzard was blowing, and the snow was staying on the streets. . . . For the rest of the day, the [German] motorized units pounded and roared over the cobblestone streets: hundreds and hundreds of vehicles plastered with snow, the faces of their occupants red with what some thought was shame but I fear was in most cases merely the cold. By evening, the occupation was complete.

Josef's brother and his family had already left Czechoslovakia for the safety of Great Britain, and now Mandula, Madeleine, and Josef were forced to flee as well. Otherwise, the Gestapo (Nazi police) would seek out Josef and arrest him for his political affiliations. While Josef and Mandula made plans to escape, they left two-year-old Madeleine with family. Trying to stay one step ahead of the Gestapo, the couple roamed the streets of Prague during the day and slept in the homes of friends at night until Josef managed to obtain the

British Prime Minister Neville Chamberlain shakes hands with Hitler after forging the Munich Pact in September 1938. In a phrase that will forever resonate with irony, Chamberlain declared that the appeasement of Germany had secured "peace in our time."

papers necessary for leaving the country.

He and Mandula quickly retrieved Madeleine, said goodbye to family members, and packed only two suitcases. At 11 o'clock that same night, they boarded a train bound for Belgrade. When they arrived, Josef sought his old friends Jara and Vlado Ribnikar. But the Korbels were no safer in Yugoslavia—the government there was pro-German. Helping the Korbels was "dangerous," Jara Ribnikar recalled years later. "There was a feeling that all diplomats were spies. But Vlado knew everybody in town and had friends in the government. He was able to get them out [of the country]."

The Korbels then traveled to Greece and on to Great Britain, where they finally met Jan Korbel and his family. For the moment, they were out of immediate danger. However, Josef and Jan's parents, as well as their sister, Margareta, and her husband and daughters, were still in Czechoslovakia. Mandula's parents had stayed behind as well. They were in great jeopardy—reports were filtering out to Western Europe that the Nazis had begun sealing Czech borders and implementing swift and brutal force against any opponents of the new regime.

As conditions worsened in Central and Eastern Europe, thousands more attempted to flee the oppression and violence of Nazi-controlled territories. Many people also risked their lives to help others escape. One such person, an Englishman named Nicholas Winton, was helping to evacuate Czech and Jewish children from Czechoslovakia. Somehow, Margareta managed to get Dagmar, one of her daughters, on one of Winton's trains out of the country.

Dagmar's journey was remarkable: at age 11, she was traveling alone across Europe to a country she had never seen, to stay with her aunt Anna (as Mandula was often called), her uncle Josef, and her little cousin Madeleine. It is not clear why Dagmar's mother, father, and younger sister, Milena, did not leave Czechoslovakia. What is clear is that Dagmar and the Korbels would spend the next six years separated from their family, friends, and homeland.

Only after Hitler invaded Poland on September 1, 1939, did Great Britain and France declare war on Germany. In less than 25 years, nearly all of Europe was once again at war. The Treaty of Versailles and the League of Nations had utterly failed to maintain peace in Europe. Those failures would have dire consequences for millions of people worldwide.

Fearful but curious, British children take shelter in a ditch during a German air raid over London in 1940.

..

4

THE WORLD IN TURMOIL: LIVING IN EXILE

After Hitler had seized what remained of Czechoslovakia in March 1939, he turned his attention to Poland. In the U.S.S.R., Joseph Stalin was becoming uneasy with Hitler's aggressive campaign, knowing that only Poland was keeping Germany from reaching his own territory. He worried that Hitler was planning an invasion of Russia.

Because of this uncertainty, when Stalin was approached by Hitler about forming a mutual nonaggression pact, he consented. On August 23, 1939, Germany and the U.S.S.R. signed a 10-year pact in which Stalin promised not to oppose a German invasion of Poland and Hitler declared that Germany would take no military action in the event of a Soviet invasion of Finland. It was later learned that the agreement also included plans to divide Poland between Germany and the U.S.S.R.

Great Britain and France had assured Poland of military aid should Hitler attempt an invasion, but Hitler believed that he could negotiate a settlement if necessary—a strategy he had used many times before. On September 1, 1939, Hitler ordered a full-scale invasion of Poland. In a lightning-quick attack now known as a

German tanks advance through what remains of Warsaw after Poland falls to Germany and the Soviet Union in September 1939. "Further successes can no longer be attained without the shedding of blood," Hitler had told his senior officers that year. "We are left with [this] decision: to attack Poland at the first suitable opportunity."

blitzkrieg, Germany battered Poland with its entire military arsenal: while air power bombed railroads, highways, harbors, factories, major cities, and munitions and supplies installations, German tanks and massive infantry support rolled across Poland's border. Rather than fight a straight-on battle and engage Polish troops, the Germans swept around them, encircled them, and ultimately overpowered them.

Honoring their agreement with Poland, Great Britain and France declared war on Germany two days later. But it was already too late. In only 19 days, Poland succumbed to the more powerful military forces of Germany. Then, under the guise of protecting his Russian countrymen in the Polish region, Stalin too invaded Poland. The secret agreement between Germany and Russia was fulfilled; Poland had been divided and was occupied by both Germany and the U.S.S.R. Stalin's forces met little resistance; in fact, many Jews and Poles, in their efforts to escape certain torture or death at the hands of the Nazis, fled into Russian-occupied areas.

Hitler continued his territorial advance the following year, when he easily overwhelmed Norway and Denmark. In May 1940, German forces swept through the Netherlands, defeating the Dutch army in only five days and Belgium by month's end. The Allies, believing that the Germans would concentrate their offensive in these countries, were unprepared for Hitler's next move.

To prevent a German invasion, France had fortified its northeastern border with an elaborate system of forts and gun emplacements known as the Maginot Line. But French military leaders failed to extend the line along the French-Belgian frontier to the sea. Breaking through the difficult but less protected terrain of the Ardennes forest, the Germans skirted the Maginot Line and poured into France. At the same time, Italy declared war on France and Great Britain. Despite valiant resistance, France was overwhelmed, and in June 1940, it surrendered to Germany and Italy. An armistice was signed on June 25 at Compiègne Forest, the very place where in 1918 Germany had surrendered to the Allies, ending World War I. Hitler was ecstatic. The humiliation of Germany's defeat 22 years before had finally been avenged. Adolf Hitler was close to realizing his dream of ruling Europe. Only Great Britain stood in his way.

Though safely out of Nazi-occupied Czechoslovakia by this time, the Korbels were well aware of Hitler's unrelenting progress. A German invasion of Great Britain seemed inevitable. In London, Czech president Beneš had set up a government in exile and Korbel, eager to take an active role in his nation's government and hoping to maintain contact with his countrymen, spearheaded the establishment of a Czech information

Eduard Beneš works from his office in London, England, where he established a Czech government in exile during World War II. Under Beneš, Josef Korbel set up an information department whose daily news broadcasts were heard by thousands in occupied Czechoslovakia.

department. He helped organize four daily radio broadcasts out of Britain through the BBC (British Broadcasting Corporation), including a half-hour news program that reached a large audience in occupied Czechoslovakia. In the *Washington Post* article "Out of the Past," published on February 9, 1997, State Department reporter Michael Dobbs quotes Ota Ornest, one of the editors of the Czech language service during the war, describing Korbel's work: "He supervised every broadcast, evaluated it, told us what was good and what was bad. He had good journalistic instincts, even though he was not a journalist by profession. He knew everybody that was worth knowing."

Madeleine Korbel was only two years old when her parents bundled her up, packed their belongings, and fled to London just weeks after the Nazi occupation of Czechoslovakia. At such a young age, she was probably unaware of the horrors of the war taking place around her. In many ways the Korbels were more fortunate than most of the political refugees who fled the German occupation. Most important, Josef had avoided arrest and imprisonment—or worse. He was also fortunate to have connected with other colleagues once he arrived in London. And though the Korbels also had to leave Czechoslovakia quickly, they had friends who helped them along the way. The Korbels also had few immediate financial concerns. Some months before the Munich Pact was signed, Josef's father, Arnost, had sold his interest in the building materials business, and the money from the sale now supported the family in exile.

Although it must have been very difficult for the Korbels to leave their home and family in such haste, they at least had been spared the terror of hearing gunfire and bomb explosions. They soon learned, however, that London provided only temporary safety from such dangers—like millions of other people throughout Great Britain, the Korbels were about to experience the war firsthand.

After the fall of France, only the narrow English Channel separated the Nazis from Great Britain and the complete occupation of Europe. Great Britain faced Germany with steely resolve. On June 17, 1940, British prime minister Winston Churchill expressed his country's determination to continue the battle: "What has happened in France makes no difference to British faith and purpose. We have become the sole champions now in arms to defend the world cause. We shall do our best to be worthy of that high honor."

In mid-July, Hitler delivered this message to his mil-

"I remember spending huge portions of my life in air-raid shelters singing 'A Hundred Green Bottles Hanging on the Wall,'" Madeleine (right, c. 1939) has said of her childhood in war-torn London, England. Having failed to defeat the Royal Air Force in 1940, the German Luftwaffe *relentlessly bombed civilian areas in an attempt to break the spirit of the British people. On facing page, London's St. Paul's Cathedral rises out of the flames and smoke of surrounding buildings.*

itary forces: "I have decided to begin to prepare for, and, if necessary, to carry out, an invasion of England." He outlined the steps necessary to meet this objective. Because Great Britain's strength lay in its air force, part one of the plan was to begin the battle in the skies. The German *Luftwaffe* (air force) was to cripple the British RAF (Royal Air Force) before launching a ground or sea attack. This way, Britain's warships would not be protected by air support when Germany crossed the channel. With a frenzied intensity, the *Luftwaffe* bombed British carrier ships in the channel and RAF air bases. The Battle of Britain had begun.

But Hitler had not anticipated that Britain's defense would be so powerful. The RAF fought valiantly; its fighter planes were far superior in maneuverability, fire power, and speed than the German airplanes. Moreover, Britain's radar and ground forces were more efficient. By the end of August the *Luftwaffe* had been defeated.

In September, hoping to terrorize the British people, Hitler turned his attention inland and ordered the bombing of cities, including London, Manchester, Nottingham, and Coventry—a direct attack on civilians.

These air raids came by day and by night. Roused from sleep or interrupted at work or play by the screaming sound of the air-raid sirens that warned of approaching enemy planes, people left their homes for the safety of underground shelters. Each raid was devastating—houses, churches, stores, schools, and other buildings were demolished, and whole city blocks were destroyed. During a BBC radio interview, one witness described the aftermath of a raid on Coventry:

> There was a mist over the town as men and women began to crawl out of their shelters, look for their friends and survey the ruins of their city. They could hardly recognise it. . . . Hardly a building remained standing. It was impossible to see where the central streets we knew so well had been. Fires were still raging in every direction and from time to time we heard the crash of a fallen roof or wall. . . . It seemed so hopeless with our homes and shops and so much of our lovely old city in ruins. You might say we were dazed.

But the British people would not let Hitler break their spirit. They dug out, buried their dead, and came away from each ruthless attack with a stronger resolve.

The Korbels moved a great deal during this time. Once the bombing raids began over London, Josef and Jan rented a house together outside the city. Eventually Josef moved his family to Walton-on-Thames, another suburb of London. But the Korbels could not escape the bombings. When asked about those years in exile, Madeleine Albright remembers seeking refuge in the air-raid shelters of Notting Hill Gate. She described the experience in an interview with *Time* magazine:

> I remember spending huge portions of my life in air-raid shelters singing "A Hundred Green Bottles Hanging on the Wall." . . . I remember when we moved to Walton-on-Thames, where they had just invented some kind of a steel table. They said if your house was bombed and you were under the table, you would survive. We had this table, and we ate on the table and we slept under the table and we played around the table.

Mandula and Josef Korbel (right, back row) pose with Madeleine (right, front row) and other family members while the Korbels were in exile in London.

After the Battle of Britain the tide of the war finally began to turn. Great Britain had stubbornly held its own, frustrating Hitler. The RAF began bombing Berlin after successfully penetrating Nazi airspace. By now, however, Hitler was obsessed with completing his "master plan" to control Europe, and millions more would die before Nazi Germany was defeated.

For some time, rumors had trickled out of central and eastern Europe that Jews and other "undesirables" were being rounded up by the thousands and transported to "concentration" or internment camps in German-occupied territories. These so-called labor camps were actually death camps, where millions of people were worked, starved, shot, or gassed to death. In the process of transmitting news to Czechs in the occupied territory, Josef Korbel undoubtedly helped to disseminate this appalling information. The world would slowly learn to its horror the names of some of the more notorious extermination camps: Auschwitz-Birkenau and Treblinka in Poland; Bergen-Belsen, Buchenwald, and Dachau in Germany; and Terezin in Czechoslovakia.

Adolf Hitler had almost as much disdain for Communists as he did for Jews. His irrational aspiration to create a "racially pure" Europe so clouded his judgment that he began making grave tactical errors. On June 22, 1941, ignoring the nonaggression pact he had signed with Stalin less than two years earlier, Hitler invaded Russia. Now German forces were fighting the war on two fronts, east and west.

Initially, Germany's surprise attack on Russia gave its forces an edge over Stalin's army. But Soviet troops, long accustomed to the frigid winters of Russia, eventually rallied, inflicting tremendous losses on the Germans. Shortly after the German invasion, the U.S.S.R. also appealed to Great Britain and the United States for military aid.

Any hope that Hitler had of victory was forever lost on December 7, 1941, a date that American president Franklin D. Roosevelt declared would "live in infamy." On that day, Japan launched an unprovoked attack on the U.S. naval base at Pearl Harbor, Hawaii, and the United States officially entered World War II.

Throughout Hitler's campaign, the United States had remained officially neutral but had nevertheless sent military officers to England as early as October 1940. The United States later agreed to provide war materials to Great Britain, and promised that if both Japan and Germany forced it into war, it would join Britain in defeating Germany first.

Japan had been taking advantage of the war in Europe to expand its own power into China and Southeast Asia. The United States imposed strict economic sanctions on Japan in an effort to prevent it from reaching its goal of dominating what it called a "Greater East

Wearing the striped uniforms of Nazi prisoners, Polish children interned in the Auschwitz concentration camp await liberation by Russian soldiers in April 1945.

Asia Co-Prosperity Sphere." In 1940, around the same time that the United States was meeting with Great Britain, Japan joined the Axis powers and moved troops into Indochina. By July 1941, President Roosevelt had cut off U.S.–Japanese trade relations. When the United States refused to lift its sanctions and allow Japan's continued expansion, Japan threatened to declare war.

On December 7, while Japanese and U.S. representatives were still negotiating, Japan launched an unprovoked attack on the U.S. military base at Pearl Harbor in Oahu, Hawaii. When the bombing was through, more than 2,300 servicemen and -women had been killed, and the U.S. naval fleet had sustained severe damage. The following day, the United States declared war on Japan. In doing so, it also declared war on Italy and Germany, though not formally. Days later, Germany declared war on the United States, which now joined Great Britain, the Soviet Union, and dozens of other countries in a united effort to defeat the Axis powers.

World War II would rage for another four years before the Allies ultimately triumphed in 1945. The stories about Nazi death camps and about the unspeakable atrocities committed against millions of Jews, political dissidents, gypsies, and homosexuals were confirmed as the Allied forces came upon one camp after another on their march toward the German capital of Berlin. In each place, the barbed-wire fences and electrified gates surrounding the camp were cut, and the prisoners— many too weak to stand—were liberated immediately.

The horror of Hitler's frenzied, genocidal obsession with "ethnic cleansing" was visible everywhere. Allied soldiers found men, women, and children riddled with disease and nearly starved to death. Millions of others were beyond rescue—the remains of human bodies lay in hastily dug mass graves scattered about the camp-grounds. Inside buildings, huge ovens, filled with human bones from mass burnings, were discovered.

More than six million Jews and other "undesirables" died in this grisly holocaust.

Even to the end, Hitler had never faltered in his passionate desire to rid the world of "inferiors." Throughout the war, his top priority had been to remove all Jews from Germany. Often, military personnel and equipment that were desperately needed in battle were instead diverted to the camps to facilitate round-the-clock extermination.

On April 30, 1945, facing defeat, capture, and certain execution for his crimes, Adolf Hitler committed suicide. In his will, he left a command to his people: "Continue to fight the Jews." Two days before Hitler's suicide, Mussolini was captured and shot while trying to flee advancing Allied forces in Italy. On August 6 and 9, the United States unleashed two atomic bombs on the Japanese cities of Hiroshima and Nagasaki; Japan surrendered on August 10.

For the second time in less than 30 years, Europe was faced with digging out from the ruins of a global war. For civilians returning from exile, nothing was certain. What would they find? Family members from whom they'd been separated for years? Their homes damaged or destroyed? Their possessions forever lost? Madeleine Korbel and her family were among the hundreds of thousands facing these concerns as they made the long pilgrimage home.

"You know the little girl in the national costume who gives flowers at the airport? I used to do that for a living," Albright says of her years in Belgrade, where the Korbels lived after the war. Dressed in a traditional Czech costume, the junior diplomat (left) poses with her governess; her sister, Katharine; and an unidentified Yugoslavian boy.

5

FREEDOM FOUND, FREEDOM LOST

fter six years in exile, the Korbels were free to return home. Only two years old when she left Czechoslovakia, Madeleine was now eight and returning to a country she barely remembered. In July 1945 she and her sister Katharine, who had been born in 1942, and her cousin Dagmar boarded a transport plane bound for Prague. Though the capital had been spared heavy destruction during the war, it was not the beautiful city that Josef and Mandula Korbel had left behind. Many necessities, like food and medical supplies, were scarce. People roamed the streets looking for food and trying to find long-lost relatives.

Dagmar's family was gone. Her parents; her sister, Milena; and her grandparents, Arnost and Olga Korbel, had all perished. Josef and Mandula told Madeleine only that her relatives had died "during the course of the war." At 17, Dagmar was an orphan. With nowhere else to go, she moved with the Korbels into a second-floor apartment at Hradčany Square in the heart of Prague.

The Czech government, led by President Beneš, had also returned home. The foreign ministry office where Josef had worked before the war was now just around the corner from the family's apartment. By this time, Josef had become a trusted associate of Beneš's, and in September 1945, Beneš appointed the 36-year-old Korbel ambassador to Yugoslavia. Josef would be returning to the country where he had lived and worked as a young attaché, but this diplomatic assignment would carry much more importance in the politics of postwar Europe.

Yugoslavia, liberated from the Nazis in 1944, was now headed by Josip Broz Tito, a passionate advocate of Communism who had served time in prison under the Austro-Hungarian Empire for his anti-monarchy beliefs and who had led an anti-Nazi guerilla unit known as the Partisans during World War II.

Czechoslovakia had also been liberated by the Communists, and though the party was not yet a dominant voice in the new democracy, it did have a large political base there. Aware of the political threat that Communism posed to his country, Beneš sought to maintain contact with—and keep watch over—the government of Yugoslavia. Korbel was the ideal man to send there. He had been well liked in Yugoslavia's political circles before the war, and Beneš knew that Korbel strongly believed, as he did, in the principles of democracy. He could be trusted to alert Beneš to any political dangers. While Dagmar stayed behind with another relative, Josef, Mandula, and their two daughters headed for the Yugoslavian capital of Belgrade.

Josef Korbel was stunned by what he saw in Belgrade. Yugoslavia had been ravaged. Nearly ten percent of the population had died during World War II, ethnic civil wars, and the Communist revolution of 1944. Thousands of villages and towns lay in ruin. He also realized to his dismay that as Czech ambassador, he was in an awkward and precarious position. As Michael Dobbs related in his 1997 *Washington Post* article:

> The Yugoslav communists did not know quite how to deal with Czechoslovakia, which had one foot in the Soviet

camp and the other in the West. [Korbel] was half friend, half enemy. He enjoyed an enviable degree of access to Tito and other senior Yugoslav officials. But his democratic, pro-Western sympathies and long London exile made him automatically suspect.

Josef tried contacting several old friends, including Vlado and Jara Ribnikar. When he finally got in touch with Jara, he discovered that she was nothing like the gentle Belgrade socialite he had once known. Instead, Jara was now toting a revolver and wearing a Yugoslav partisan uniform. During the Nazi occupation, she had become one of Tito's resistance fighters and spent most of the war battling the Germans. Following this meeting, Josef and Jara never saw one another again.

Most of Korbel's other prewar friends kept their distance from him as well—it was unsafe for them to be seen with a foreign politician. Capitalists and believers in democracy were considered the enemies of Tito's Communist regime.

After having liberated many Eastern European countries from Nazi occupation, the Soviet Union began setting up "satellite" Communist governments. Among the nations that fell under its control were Poland, Bulgaria, Romania, Albania, Yugoslavia, and East Germany (Germany had been divided into four sectors by the Allied powers; the United States, Great Britain, and France combined their zones to create West Germany). These "people's democracies," as Stalin called them, were under Soviet rule and would receive military and diplomatic support from the Soviet Union. But Tito did not intend for Yugoslavia to be absorbed into the "socialist family" of the Soviet Union, and by 1948 he was being accused of not conforming with the official Soviet government.

At the time, Madeleine Korbel and her family lived in a comfortable apartment within the opulent, palatial Czech embassy in Belgrade. Josef wished to shelter his

Ten-year-old Madeleine in Switzerland, where she attended boarding school. The following year, a communist takeover of Czechoslovakia forced the Korbels to become refugees once again.

daughters from Communist propaganda, so he had hired a governess and arranged for private tutoring. When Madeleine was 10, her parents sent her to a boarding school in Switzerland. Already fluent in Czech and English (one published story reported that Madeleine, wanting to be "just like the Brits," had formed a cockney accent while living in England), she also became well versed in French. Albright now claims that learning a third language was a necessity, not an extravagance: "[I]n order to eat, I learned to speak French," she later recalled.

Madeleine's upbringing was very different from that of most children her age. She has said that the one aspect of her childhood she remembers most is that the family was constantly going somewhere. In moving so often, she learned how to adapt to a multitude of environments and developed an ease in difficult situations, such as meeting people and making new friends. In many ways, Madeleine's developing personality showed her parents' influence, particularly her mother's. Mandula had grown up living in comfort with a prosperous family. Like her daughter, she had been educated in private schools in Switzerland. From Mandula, Madeleine learned how to be flexible and how to pack up one's belongings and move on to a new place where one would have to adapt to the customs and language of an unfamiliar country.

When Madeleine returned to Belgrade during vacation breaks from school, she often played the role of "daddy's little diplomat," greeting dignitaries who visited her father. She was starting her diplomatic training early. Through this exposure to her father's world, Madeleine learned how well respected he was and how important his job was to the Czech government.

Josef Korbel was a conservative, well-disciplined intellectual, a master of protocol and of the skills required to be a successful politician. According to accounts from his children, he was also a strict father, a throwback to the old European way of raising a family. Routines were rigorously followed; his children were expected to be on time for dinner, to complete their studies each day, and to obey the instructions of their parents at all times. In school, at home, in everything Madeleine did, it seemed, she was striving for the same levels of distinction, morality, and discipline that she saw and respected in her father.

Living in Yugoslavia provided Josef with the opportunity to observe the evolution of a Communist country. Communism usually takes hold, he observed, in one of two ways: by military conquest or by an internal uprising or revolution. Once political control has been achieved, the whole structure of a country's society is revamped. Almost every facet of the lives of its citizens

Communist demonstrators march through a Czech city street carrying huge portraits of President Klement Gottwald and Soviet dictator Joseph Stalin. Gottwald assumed power after Eduard Beneš resigned in June 1948.

is affected—their finances, politics, social relations, even their occupations. Most vital businesses, including agriculture, industry, and transportation (farms, factories, and railroads, for example) are seized from private owners by the government.

Josip Broz Tito consolidated his power in classic fashion: by "nationalizing" factories and confiscating agricultural enterprises. Political opponents were arrested and imprisoned. "Marshal" Tito exercised the same strong-arm tactics in Yugoslavia that had been employed by Stalin in Russia: any opposition to the government party was crushed. Resisters were silenced, and the press was censored. Organized religion and worship services were banned. All human thoughts and actions, it seemed, were monitored by the Communist Party. A rebel among Communists, Tito also flaunted his power and prominence among other Eastern bloc countries.

On return trips to Prague, Josef Korbel reported on the progress of Tito's Communist solidification. It appeared as though similar activities were underway in Czechoslovakia, threatening the fragile democracy of that country: after free elections were held there in the spring of 1946, Beneš continued to serve as president in the all-party government, but more votes were cast (about 38 percent) for the Communists than for any other political party. Czechoslovakia's new prime minister, Klement Gottwald, became the first Communist in that country to hold such a high government position.

In 1948, after refusing to sign a series of unfavorable trade agreements, Yugoslavia broke all ties with the Soviet Union. In a letter Tito sent to Moscow to announce his decision, he wrote: "No matter how much each of us loves the land of socialism, the U.S.S.R., he can, in no case, love his own country less." Although this development was unnerving for Josef Korbel and his family, Tito's break with the Soviet Union was less ominous than the escalation of Communist power taking place in Czechoslovakia.

Josef knew that his pro-democracy beliefs would once again place his family in grave danger should the Communists gain control of the Czech government. Just as he and his wife and daughters had fled from the Nazis, they would now have to escape from the Communists.

Korbel expressed his concerns to Beneš, but to no avail. The president, certain that the Czech military was behind him, was not concerned about a coup d'etat (violent takeover) of the government. He still believed that Czechoslovakia was the "bridge between East and West," maintaining friendly relations with both the Soviet Union and the democratic countries of Western Europe. Sadly, he misjudged his support.

In February 1948, the Communists, already in con-

An avenue to freedom: Josef Korbel (second from right) with other members of a United Nations delegation en route to India to help settle a territorial dispute in July 1948. Korbel's position as a U.N. representative allowed him to travel to America, where he eventually applied for political asylum.

trol of the Czech police force, staged a coup. The ailing Beneš eventually agreed to demands to create a new, Communist-dominated government.

Suddenly, the Korbels, particularly Josef, were once again unsafe in their homeland. For the second time in nine years, they were forced to flee political persecution. However, this time Josef wouldn't have to hide until he could obtain false papers to secure his family's escape. Vladimir Clementis, the deputy foreign minister of the Communist-run government, offered Korbel a position as the Czech representative in a United

Nations delegation to settle a territorial dispute between India and Pakistan. This meant that eventually Korbel would have to travel to America, where the United Nations is headquartered.

No one knows for certain why Clementis, who knew that Korbel was an advocate of democracy, would give him such an opportunity. But for Madeleine and her family, the appointment meant taking another long journey. With her mother; sister; infant brother, John; and later her father, Madeleine would find freedom on the shores of the United States of America.

The Statue of Liberty, a symbol of independence and opportunity for millions of immigrants to America.

6

HELLO, LADY LIBERTY

To understand how a refugee views America after having lived under tyranny and oppression, one must first understand what the promise of life in America means to those who come here. In the United States, the very foundation of democracy rests on the principal belief that all people have a right to "life, liberty, and the pursuit of happiness." Even before America was founded, travelers from several European countries, especially Spain, France, and Great Britain, launched expeditions to discover new frontiers where they could not only acquire wealth but also find the religious and political freedom that they did not have in their own countries.

The United States has welcomed more than 60 million immigrants to its shores since records began to be kept in 1820. Each person has brought different skills and ideas to a country whose founding fathers aimed to create a government that would protect the liberty of its citizens. The U.S. Constitution includes the guarantee of certain "inalienable rights"—freedom of speech, religion, political beliefs, and the press. What better place for the Korbels to live?

In New York Harbor sits Liberty Island (formerly known as Bedloe's Island), the site of an immense statue that has come to represent American liberty. Its proper name is *Liberty Enlightening the World*, but most of us know it as the Statue of Liberty. Within the safety of this harbor, it towers 152 feet above the water, a beacon for millions of immigrants arriving in America.

The Statue of Liberty was a gift from France in 1884 to commemorate the alliance of the two countries in the American Revolution. Lady Liberty is full of symbolism; she has been described as "a proud woman dressed in a loose robe that falls in graceful folds. . . . The right arm holds a great torch raised high in the air. The left arm grasps a tablet bearing the date of the Declaration of Independence. A crown with huge spikes, like sun rays, rests on her head. At the feet is a broken shackle . . . symbolizing the overthrow of tyranny."

For many Europeans who emigrated between 1891 and 1920, seeing the Statue of Liberty meant that they had reached the end of their journey. American author Emma Lazarus, so moved by the suffering—and hopefulness—of countless Jewish refugees who poured into New York around the turn of the century, wrote a poem called "The New Colossus," which describes the meaning of freedom to those who have been oppressed. The poem, inscribed on the base of the statue's pedestal, reads in part:

> "Give me your tired, your poor,
> Your huddled masses yearning to breathe free,
> The wretched refuse of your teeming shore.
> Send these, the homeless, tempest-tost to me.
> I lift my lamp beside the golden door!"

Mandula Korbel and her children were among the thousands of immigrants who saw the Statue of Liberty as they arrived by boat from a Europe still struggling to overcome the devastation of World War II. When the Korbels arrived in New York in late 1948, they finally felt free.

After completing his work in Pakistan, Josef Korbel joined his family in America, requesting political asylum upon his arrival. Political freedom was a dream come true for Madeleine's father. No longer would he have to worry about his safety or that of his family. Amid the joy of having achieved this freedom, however, was the sad realization that he would never be able to return to his homeland while the Communists were in control. When he requested asylum in the United States, Korbel wrote on his application, "I cannot . . . return to the communist Czechoslovakia as I would be arrested for my faithful adherence to the ideals of democracy."

In fact, about four months after the Korbels arrived in the United States, the Czech court officially confiscated all of the family's property. Recent reports have suggested that Josef Korbel was tried *in absentia* (while absent) and convicted of treason, and that he would have been arrested and executed had he returned to Czechoslovakia. To date, however, no official records have been found that confirm these reports.

Once again, the Korbels had departed just in time. The new Czech government was aggressively pursuing those who seemed to pose a threat or voiced opposition to the new regime, including many of Korbel's old associates in the foreign ministry office in Prague. The Iron Curtain (a term used to describe the self-imposed isolation of Communist countries in Central and Eastern Europe) was sealing all political borders from outside influence by noncommunist countries. Madeleine's cousin Dagmar, now in her twenties, had not made the trip to America with the Korbels and was effectively trapped in Communist Europe. From that time on, Dagmar's life would be very different from that of her young cousins.

Through the end of 1948, Josef Korbel continued to work with the U.N. delegation on the Kashmir land dispute between India and Pakistan. Madeleine attended a public grade school in Great Neck, New York.

Madeleine inherited her passionate interest in international affairs from her father (shown above at the University of Denver). Of her tenure as president of the international relations club at Kent School for Girls (center, facing page), she has said, "I tortured my classmates and made them come to meetings."

Now in the sixth grade, she did not suffer from the language difficulties many other immigrant children face because she had learned English while living in London. By all appearances, Madeleine was adjusting very well to her new life and home in America.

The Korbels would move once again in early 1949, after Josef accepted a position teaching international relations at the University of Denver in Colorado. Josef packed up the family's belongings in their green Ford, and they headed west, moving into a small faculty housing apartment on Denver's South Madison Street. Although Madeleine was nearly 12 years old, she had never lived in any one place for more than a few years at a time. In Denver, she would finally put down roots.

At the University of Denver, Josef Korbel established

the Graduate School for International Studies and became its first dean. As most university professors do, he also wrote books; among them are *Tito's Communism* (1951) and *Twentieth-Century Czechoslovakia*, published in 1976, a year before his death.

Josef and Mandula enrolled their eldest daughter in the exclusive Kent School for Girls (now known as the Kent Denver School). At first she resisted going and accepting the scholarship she'd been awarded, but she ultimately received an excellent education. Always a serious student, Madeleine founded an international relations club and made herself its president. In her remarks to a "welcome home" crowd of more than 600 at the Kent Denver School in May 1997, Albright made light of her seriousness while enrolled there:

The 1955 graduating class of Kent School for Girls. Madeleine Korbel is in the front row, second from left.

I tortured my classmates and made them come to meetings. I won the United Nations contest [in the eighth grade] because I memorized, alphabetically, all 51 countries that were U.N. members. I couldn't do that now. There are 185 members.

By the time Madeleine was in high school, she had become a typical—but obedient—teenager. Her father, however, continued to be a "strict European parent," according to Madeleine's brother, John Korbel. State Department reporter Michael Dobbs described Madeleine's relationship with her father: "As she came of age, Albright consciously molded herself after her father. She was a loyal daughter who practically never rebelled against his wishes."

Albright, however, has often recounted one of the few instances when she did challenge her father.

Madeleine's invitation to her senior prom sparked a family argument over whether she would be permitted to ride with her date in his car. As a compromise, Josef agreed to let her ride with the boy—but he insisted on following them in his own car and then driving his daughter home after the dance. "My parents were obviously very serious people, very oriented toward doing the right thing," Albright said in a September 1997 interview with *Vogue* magazine.

Instead of discussing topics of interest to most teens, such as sports or social activities, Madeleine and her father talked endlessly about international affairs. Many of the papers she wrote in high school covered subjects

Madeleine (fifth from left, behind table) with other staff members of the Wellesley News. *Although she seriously considered a career in journalism, Secretary of State Albright has said that she is "very lucky, because I would have been a lousy reporter and I think I am pretty good at what I do now."*

Madeleine at her college graduation in 1959.

like the politics of India and Eastern Europe. "They are very similar in many ways," Albright's daughter Anne says of her mother and grandfather. "My mother, like my grandfather, is very intellectual, very rational. She got her sense of integrity from him."

Madeleine was one of 16 women in the 1955 graduating class of Kent Denver School. She received an academic scholarship to Wellesley College, an exclusive women's school in Massachusetts. During her four years there, she not only continued to share her father's passion for international studies but also developed an interest in journalism. And she remained an independent thinker—on a predominantly Republican campus, for example, she was one of the few students to campaign for Democratic presidential candidate Adlai Stevenson in 1956. Her extracurricular activities included editing the school newspaper.

Contemplating a career in journalism, Madeleine spent the summer between her sophomore and junior years as an intern with the *Denver Post*, covering weddings and working in the morgue (the company's file room). There she met journalist Joseph Medill Patterson Albright, a member of a prominent American publishing family whose properties included the *New York Daily News* and *Newsday*. In 1959, three days after she graduated with honors from Wellesley with a bachelor's degree in political science, Madeleine Korbel and Joseph Albright were married. Madeleine was about to embark on a new journey, filled with limitless possibilities, in her adopted homeland.

Madeleine Albright with newborn twins, Anne and Alice, in 1961.

7

THE MANY ROLES OF MADELEINE

The newlyweds first headed to Rolla, Missouri, where Joe Albright was stationed at an army base. Still seeking a position as a journalist, Madeleine worked briefly for the *Daily News*, the town's local paper. Not long after, however, Joe accepted a job at the *Chicago Sun-Times* and the couple moved to that city. There Madeleine's journalism career, only barely begun, came to an abrupt end. In a 1991 interview with Molly Sinclair of the *Washington Post*, Albright recalled the conversation she had with her husband's editor when she attempted to get a job in the field:

> He said, "Honey, what are you planning to do [for a living]?" And I said, "I am planning to be a reporter." . . . And he said, "Guild regulations will prohibit you from having a job at the *Sun-Times* and our general feeling about a spouse working at a competitive newspaper will prevent you from getting a job at another newspaper, so honey, why don't you think of another career?"

It was 1960, and the women's liberation movement, which focused on securing equal opportunities for women in the workplace, had not yet taken form. At Madeleine's own college graduation ceremony just a year and half earlier, a speaker had told the all-female class of seniors that their primary role was to raise the next generation of educated Americans. Now in Chicago and determined to establish herself as a professional in her own right, Madeleine joined the public relations staff of Encyclopedia Britannica.

Years later, shortly before being appointed the first female secretary of state, Madeleine reflected on the changing social conditions that eventually led to greater opportunities for working women. "I went to a women's college," she told Molly Sinclair, "and at a time when people were interested in advancing women, I had the right credentials." In 1960, already somewhat ahead of her time—and ahead of many of her female contemporaries—Madeleine aspired to have a family *and* a career. But she decided to put her professional plans on hold while Joe was building his career.

If any part of Madeleine's adult life reminded her of her childhood, it was when the Albrights moved three times in the first eight years of their marriage. From Chicago the couple moved to Long Island, New York, where Joe had been named city editor of *Newsday*, a paper owned by his aunt, Alicia Patterson.

In June 1961, Madeleine gave birth to twin daughters, Anne and Alice. They were six weeks premature and spent almost two months in hospital incubators. Madeleine felt helpless; she could only watch and wait for her tiny children to grow stronger and healthier. Always interested in international studies, she threw herself into an intensive eight-week, eight-hour-a-day Russian language study class to distract herself from worrying about the twins.

Madeleine's responsibilities naturally multiplied after the girls were released from the hospital. The twins were feeding three times a night, and caring for them during the day was all-consuming. Her life as a wife and mother left little time for other pursuits. Then one day, a thought occurred to Madeleine. "I kind of sat there

during the day, feeding [the twins], watching soap operas, and I thought, I didn't go to college to do this," she told Julia Reed of *Vogue* magazine. Her love of scholarship renewed by her recent Russian studies, Madeleine enrolled in graduate school at New York's Columbia University.

In 1967 a third daughter, Katharine, was born to the Albrights. By now, Madeleine had become quite adept at balancing family responsibilities with her studies. Although the Albrights had housekeepers to help with their three daughters, Madeleine herself took care of most household duties like cooking, grocery shopping, and car pooling. She rose very early each day to work on her master's thesis, *The Soviet Diplomatic Service:*

During the early years of her marriage to Joseph Patterson Albright, Madeleine delayed pursuing a profession while her husband established a career in publishing. Here, the Albrights speak with Robert Downing (center) of the Lincoln Center's Repertory Theater during a 1964 book and author luncheon.

By the time her daughter Katharine ("Katie") was born in 1967, Madeleine Albright was well on her way to earning a master's degree and had become skilled at balancing the demands of family and academic life. "As a working mother, she's got fabulous juggling skills," her daughter Anne has said.

Profile of an Elite, then woke the twins and got them off to school. Her hard work paid off—in 1968 she received a master's degree in public law and government and a certificate from the Russian Institute of Columbia University.

Not long after, Madeleine headed back to Columbia to begin working toward a Ph.D. She now thought that she would become a professor. But before year's end, she was packing and moving again, this time to Washington, D.C., where Joe was appointed news bureau chief for *Newsday*.

Madeleine was stunned. Once again, she felt pressure to put aside her own aspirations in support of her husband's career. But this time she would not be deterred. She continued her Ph.D. work long-distance by telephone with her advisor, Professor Seweryn Bialer, and her other professors, including Zbigniew Brzezinski, making trips to New York whenever possible.

Like Josef Korbel, Brzezinski was a passionate intellectual. He had grown up listening to the stories told by his parents about life in Warsaw, Poland, under a totalitarian regime. From the start, Brzezinski and Albright felt that they shared a common personal history, that they were kindred spirits from Eastern Europe. Both understood too well the sacrifices made by their parents to provide them with lives free from oppression. Albright became a favorite student of Brzezinski's, and their close professional relationship would later serve Albright well in her career.

Working on a Ph.D. while caring for three children would have been considered quite enough to handle by most of Albright's contemporaries in Georgetown, the section of Washington, D.C., where the Albrights lived. But not by Madeleine. When asked to join the board of Beauvoir, the private school her daughters attended, she obliged. Although she knew nothing about fundraising, she was put in charge of Beauvoir's annual giving drive.

Madeleine Albright was an unusual mother. Unlike many mothers in the early 1970s, she did not opt to stay home and concentrate solely on raising her children. But Albright's daughter Anne, now an attorney living near Washington, D.C., says that she never felt deprived of attention even though her mother worked and was a part-time student. "I always thought my mother's work was very exciting, and my sisters and I never felt that she didn't have enough time for us," Anne said. "She's always done the ordinary things that mothers do: getting us up in the mornings and ready for school, helping us with our homework. . . . On Fridays she would do the grocery shopping while my sisters and I were horseback riding or taking ballet class or guitar lessons. We had a wonderful life." In fact, Albright's tight schedule often required that she sit with her daughters and work on her dissertation while they did their own schoolwork.

Albright observes that women who raise families often don't have the opportunity to pursue a direct career path. "[W]omen's careers don't go in straight lines," she has said. "They zigzag all over the place." Events and decisions outside one's own control often affect the route that one's career path will take; this is especially true for women who are also mothers. In Madeleine Albright's case, this worked to her advantage. During her volunteer duties at the Beauvoir School, she met the fundraiser's cochairman, who worked in the office of Senator Edmund Muskie of Maine. Impressed by her hard work and outgoing personality, the man asked Albright to cochair a fundraiser to finance the senator's 1972 bid for the presidency.

Muskie did not receive the nomination, but Albright gained invaluable experience working for the campaign, and she made important contacts with members of the national Democratic party. Albright also gained new friends in Muskie and his wife, Jane, and the three kept in touch. Muskie called upon Madeleine again in 1975

Albright's entry into national politics began with a fundraising campaign for the Beauvoir School, a private academy that her daughters attended. She is shown here conferring with Beauvoir School principal Frances R. Borders in the early 1970s.

to help raise money for his senate reelection campaign. He won easily. Muskie's longtime chief of staff, Leon Billings, remembered Albright's work in the 1972 and 1975 campaigns. Slowly and methodically, Albright was establishing her credentials, building a network with the political "who's who" of Washington.

Albright spent eight years earning her Ph.D. in political science. She says that the hardest thing she ever did was to write her doctoral dissertation, which examines the role of the press during the "Prague Spring," the 1968 revolution in Czechoslovakia that was suppressed by Soviet troops.

While researching her dissertation, Albright spoke to many Czech journalists and writers who were willing to share their own experiences in the uprising, including Jiri Dienstbier, a chief correspondent for Prague radio. Albright and Dienstbier spent hours reviewing the events surrounding the Prague Spring. As with many others whom she'd met during her years in Washington, Madeleine kept in touch with Dienstbier even after he returned to Czechoslovakia and became the country's foreign minister in 1989. Dienstbier later introduced Albright to Václav Havel, the head of the new Czech Republic.

Under her old ally Billings's direction, Madeleine Albright landed her first paying political job working as chief legislative assistant to Senator Muskie. It was a low-level job, but Albright made the most of her opportunity. Muskie had the well-earned reputation of being the most difficult senator on Capitol Hill to work for. Some staffers were even known to hide from Muskie on occasion—but not Albright. "That she could put up with [Muskie's] temper actually served to make Muskie perceive Madeleine as more of a peer than a staffer," Billings recalled. "In an office that was always scrambling as the senator seemed to live crisis to crisis, Albright never, ever lost her sense of humor."

Albright's credentials and background in foreign policy studies certainly helped move her career along, but her diligence and persistence also impressed her colleagues. In typical Madeleine fashion, she handled every task thoroughly. Her work ethic opened professional doors that under other circumstances might have remained closed to her. Albright's own words reflect her belief in hard work: "Whatever job you have to do, do it well, because people remember. Even if you're not making foreign policy, people remember the job you did."

Senator Muskie shared Madeleine Albright's enthusiasm for foreign relations issues, and he needed an advisor who not only was proficient in handling such issues but also worked well with him. In a short period

In addition to her father, Albright counts the late senator Edmund Muskie (shown here with Albright in 1980) and former National Security Council advisor Zbigniew Brzezinski (facing page, in 1997) among the greatest intellectual influences in her life.

of time, Albright was promoted from legislative assistant to legislative director and finally to chief foreign policy advisor for Muskie. What is perhaps most remarkable about her quick ascent is that, in an era when most political positions open to women were entry-level, Albright—just shy of her 40th birthday—had broken into the predominantly male field of American policy-making.

In 1978, Zbigniew Brzezinski, who had been named National Security Council advisor to President Jimmy Carter, offered Albright a job as congressional liaison at the NSC. It was a natural step up for her. The position

would mean more prestige and responsibility—and would place Albright directly in the center of the national political arena.

It also presented a challenge of a different sort. It was widely known that Muskie and Brzezinski did not see eye to eye on many foreign-policy issues and did not particularly like one another. But Albright, who greatly respected and admired both men, had long since honed the diplomatic skills necessary to avoid conflicts between the senator and the national security advisor and to make them both feel comfortable working with her.

If the 1970s were productive for Albright, the 1980s would test her resiliency both personally and professionally. When Carter lost the 1980 presidential election to Republican Ronald Reagan, Albright suddenly found herself out of a job. Desiring to keep abreast of new academic developments in her discipline, she participated in—and won—an international competition for a fellowship from the Woodrow Wilson International Center for Scholars.

With the fellowship money, she wrote *Poland: The Role of the Press in Political Change* (1983). The book, which includes a forward by her friend and colleague Zbigniew Brzezinski, is similar in scope to her Ph.D. dissertation. Albright examined the role of the press in Poland's Solidarity movement, which began in 1980. "The press, in a sense, is the mouthpiece of legitimacy; the organ through which a Communist regime seeks to justify itself and its behavior to its citizens," Albright wrote in her introduction. "When the press sounds an uncertain trumpet, this legitimacy comes into question."

While writing her book, Albright was also a senior fellow in Soviet and Eastern European Affairs at the Center for Strategic and International Studies. There, she examined political trends in the Soviet Union and other Eastern European countries.

Although her career was advancing smoothly, Albright's home life was a different story. Her world was temporarily shattered one day in 1982, when Joe came home and announced that their 23-year marriage was over. It was an utter surprise to Madeleine.

Years later, during an interview on the TV news program *60 Minutes*, Ed Bradley asked her what her greatest setback had been. Albright responded, "I must say, [it] was my divorce—in that I had not expected it. I had expected to continue in what I was doing and live happily ever after." Did the divorce change her in any way? Bradley asked. "No," she responded, but added, "I think it made me more self-reliant, though. I think if it taught me anything, it was to rely on my own judgment and to do what I needed to do for my daughters and for myself."

As devastating as her divorce had been, Madeleine refused to let her career suffer. The same year her mar-

riage ended, she was appointed to the faculty of Georgetown University, where she became director of the Women in Foreign Service program and research professor of international affairs in the School of Foreign Service. While there, she implemented programs that stressed career opportunities for women in foreign affairs.

As a professor, Albright was outgoing and engaging, and her enthusiasm was contagious. Though characterized as demanding by some of her students, she was also considered a phenomenal professor. She was always well prepared for her lectures and translated complicated course material into relevant, easy-to-understand information. At a time when the U.S.S.R. was disintegrating and the political borders of its satellite countries

Madeleine Albright with her mother, Mandula Korbel, and daughters Anne and Alice at Katie's high school graduation. "My mom never told us, you should do this or you should do that," Anne said in 1997. "Nevertheless, academic achievement was highly valued in our family."

seemed to change daily, Albright was known to carry her lesson plans under one arm and a clutch of national and international newspapers under the other arm.

Occasionally, Albright even invited her students to her home for weekend retreats, where she would engage them in open discussions about current international affairs. Extremely popular with her students, she was showered with awards and accolades during her 11-year tenure at Georgetown—including the honor of Teacher of the Year four years running.

During her years at Georgetown University, the White House remained Republican (Ronald Reagan served two terms; George Bush served one). Undeterred, Madeleine Albright created a virtual think-tank of Democratic foreign policy–makers by inviting many of them to her home for dinner parties, where international issues were freely discussed and where her guests could exchange ideas. Albright's gatherings attracted an impressive group of politicians, and she made sure to forge relationships with all she met. No one knew who might show up on a given evening, so the debate was always lively.

One summer evening in 1988, Albright met a young governor from Arkansas who had been selected to deliver the keynote speech that July during the Democratic National Convention in New York. His name was Bill Clinton, and he was a friend of Chuck Manatt, an important figure in the Democratic Party. Manatt and Albright were close friends, and when he called to say that he would be bringing Clinton by her house that evening, she knew that he must have thought highly of the governor.

After dinner, Albright, Manatt, Clinton, and perhaps a dozen other guests discussed a variety of topics, including the Iran-Contra investigation, the continued demise of Communism in central and eastern Europe, and who would be named George Bush's running mate in the upcoming presidential election. Clinton proved an able contributor of opinions on these serious topics, but he also talked about music—about playing the saxophone and the styles of jazz greats Dave Brubeck and Stan Getz. The governor was articulate on many subjects and very comfortable in the high-powered political environment of Washington. Albright was impressed.

Clinton also understood proper protocol, and he sent Albright a thank-you note for the dinner and dialogue. Thus began a casual correspondence between the two. In one of his letters, Clinton asked Albright to recommend him for membership in the Council on Foreign Relations. After he provided her with a 120-page essay detailing his thoughts on specific international issues, Albright was more than satisfied that Clinton was well informed on appropriate subjects. Without reservation, she endorsed his nomination to the council.

Bill Clinton was one of many political figures who sought Albright's counsel and insight on foreign-relations matters. During her 12 years of involvement in international affairs—as legislative aide, congressional liaison, research professor, and foreign policy advisor— every Democrat who aspired to occupy the Oval Office of the White House eventually stopped by Albright's house for advice.

As a break from the classroom and in an effort to keep current in her field, Albright continued to seek new outlets for discussion and research. She attended the Georgetown Leadership Seminar, a week-long program offered each summer by Georgetown University in which officials of foreign governments attended sessions with members of the U.S. State Department and the Pentagon. In 1989, Albright accepted the post of president of the Center for National Policy, a nonprofit organization comprised of professionals in government, industry, labor, and education who are devoted to the study of domestic and international issues.

Within only a few months, Albright's abilities as both an executive and an administrator had turned the

Students of the Georgetown School of Foreign Service bid farewell to their favorite professor in January 1993, after Madeleine Albright was confirmed as U.S. Permanent Representative to the United Nations. "Students flocked to her," said Peter Krogh, the dean who hired Albright. "She was like a pied piper."

Center into one of the most comprehensive, up-to-date foreign-policy information hubs in Washington. Albright's reputation among Washington politicians was quickly growing.

On November 3, 1992, Bill Clinton—the young governor whom Albright had first met four years earlier—was elected the 42nd president of the United States. After 12 years of Republican domination, a Democrat was once again in the White House. Clinton promised to assemble a cabinet composed of a diverse group of people, one "that reflected America."

He had not forgotten Madeleine Albright, whom he believed was the natural choice for the new United States permanent representative to the United Nations.

After Clinton announced her nomination during a press conference in December 1992, Albright expressed how honored she felt to have earned this position: "As a result of the generous spirit of the American people, our family had the privilege of growing up as free Americans," she declared. "You can therefore understand how proud I will be to sit at the United Nations behind the nameplate that says UNITED STATES OF AMERICA."

For Madeleine Albright, the journey from Czech refugee to wife, mother, student, professor, and foreign-policy advisor had been possible only in America. Through hard work and determination, she had overcome every obstacle in her path. Now she would represent the United States around the globe.

Ambassador Albright conducts a news conference in August 1993 on U.S. involvement in Bosnia.

8

OLIVE BRANCHES EMBRACING THE WORLD

Since wars begin in the minds of men, it is in the minds of men that the defenses of peace must be constructed.

—from the constitution of the United Nations Educational,
Scientific, and Cultural Organization

During most of Madeleine Albright's life, she was exposed to international affairs in one way or another. She lived foreign policy as a refugee from oppression, studied and taught it as a scholar and professor, and nurtured its development as an advisor to politicians and diplomats. As the new United States permanent representative to the United Nations, she would have the chance to be an architect of its future. And because President Clinton elevated the U.N. ambassador post to cabinet status—and because she would be a member of the National Security Council—Ambassador Albright would be a vital link in the new administration's foreign policy team.

Albright's job at the United Nations was steeped in history. It originated after World War II, when the nations of the world had a strong desire to ensure that they would never again have to

A representative of China is the first to sign the United Nations charter in June 1945, four months before the charter is ratified and the U.N. becomes an official international organization (above). Nearly 50 years later, in 1994, U.S. Ambassador Madeleine Albright (facing page) leads a United Nations Security Council meeting on Somalia.

engage in a war of such proportions and with such catastrophic consequences. The League of Nations, the well-intentioned organization formed after World War I, had failed to prevent the political and military reemergence of Germany and the rise of Japan. In 1945, with the guns of World War II silent and the tanks finally still, it was imperative to try once again to create an international organization that would work to secure lasting peace and foster international cooperation. Thus, the United Nations was established.

The phrase "united nations" was actually coined by President Franklin Roosevelt during World War II to

describe the Allies' common goal of defeating the Axis powers. As early as 1940, the Allies had begun to plan for the political aftereffects of the war: Roosevelt envisioned an organization in which the primary responsibility for assuring international peace would be shouldered by the "Big Four"—the United States, Great Britain, China, and the U.S.S.R. This alliance led to a more comprehensive global organization, called the United Nations. Representatives of 50 nations signed the United Nations charter in San Francisco on June 26, 1945. (Poland became the 51st member shortly thereafter.) This charter was ratified on October 24, 1945—that date is now celebrated as United Nations Day. Today, 185 countries are members of the organization.

The United Nations charter is comprised of 111

"articles," rules that define the organization's goals and the means by which these goals should be achieved. Among its articles are pledges to "save humanity from the scourge of war"; "protect human rights and the equal rights of men and women and of nations large and small"; "promote justice and respect for international law"; and "promote social progress, better standards of life, and freedom."

The permanent headquarters of the United Nations rests on a tract of land near New York City's East River. The land was donated by John D. Rockefeller Jr. Although the U.N. headquarters is located in America, its land and buildings are considered international territory. The U.N. functions as a self-contained entity, with its own flag, post office, and postage stamps. Its emblem is a globe embraced by olive branches, the universal sign for peace. In all, six official languages are spoken at the U.N.: Arabic, Chinese, English, French, Russian, and Spanish.

In its purest sense, the United Nations is the world's town hall, where "citizens" from all continents engage in ongoing dialogue and planning and where they can bring grievances or disputes for discussion and resolution. Here all nations are equal; each has a voice and a vote in determining the course of action on any given issue. For this reason, the strength and effectiveness of the U.N. depends upon the cooperation and support of its members. It does not, however, make laws, and its decisions are not binding on any government.

The United Nations also provides humanitarian assistance to the world's countries through programs like UNICEF (the Children's Fund). It provides food, medicine, clothing, and volunteers to help developing countries improve the quality of life for their children and combat problems such as disease, malnutrition, and illiteracy.

The United Nations is made up of six components: the General Assembly, the Security Council, the Eco-

nomic and Social Council, the Trusteeship Council, the International Court of Justice, and the Secretariat. The General Assembly is the heart of the United Nations; all members are represented there. The assembly convenes from mid-September to mid-December each year. According to a U.N. guidebook, on any given day, a visitor to an assembly session might hear about "plans for action against pollution of the air and seas . . . measures to improve conditions of international trade . . . proposals for new disarmament measures . . . principles of international law . . . [or] violations of human rights." Though the assembly has no powers of enforcement, it can make recommendations to other U.N. bodies regarding any matter brought to its attention.

Another U.N. body, the Security Council, is responsible for helping to uphold world peace and security. By

As ambassador to the United Nations, Albright drew attention not only to the organization's humanitarian efforts abroad but also to its work in America. Here she reads a U.N.-sponsored story to an ailing New Jersey child as part of President Clinton's 1993 Thanksgiving weekend campaign to honor American health-care workers.

charter, all U.N. member nations agree to abide by and carry out the decisions of the Security Council. The Council is comprised of five permanent members—the United States, Great Britain, France, China, and Russia—and 10 nonpermanent members, who are elected by the General Assembly to two-year terms. The presidency of the council rotates each month, in alphabetical order of its member countries.

The Security Council can meet anywhere and at any time, especially when peace somewhere in the world is threatened. As with the General Assembly, each member of the council has one vote. Nine votes carry the majority on most procedural matters, such as the election of a new secretary-general or admission of a new member to the U.N. However, on issues of critical importance, such as the deployment of U.N. peace-keeping forces, the five permanent members must be among those nine votes before action is taken.

The Security Council may take action in two ways: by investigating or mediating disputes between countries and then defining the terms for a peaceful resolution, or by implementing more drastic measures—severing diplomatic relations, imposing economic sanctions, expelling a member from the U.N., or even threatening to use or actually using military force. After the Gulf War of 1991, for example, the Security Council imposed severe economic sanctions upon Iraq. These sanctions will be lifted only after Iraq complies with the resolutions for peace set forth by the United Nations Security Council.

Three other organs of the U.N. are the Economic and Social Council, which focuses on economic growth, upholding human rights, and sharing developments in science and technology; the International Court of Justice or World Court, the judicial arm of the U.N. that presides over matters of international law, such as border disputes; and the Trusteeship Council, which was established to help dependent territories work toward self-government or independence.

The sixth body, known as the Secretariat, is the administrative branch of the United Nations. Its staff of about 5,000 is composed primarily of men and women from the member states who handle most of the behind-the-scenes daily operations for the organization. The Secretariat includes office administrators, linguists, public relations staffers, security personnel, librarians, journalists, and tour guides. And because these employees remain citizens of their native countries, each must take an oath promising to serve only the interests of the U.N. while working and not to be influenced by the needs or desires of his or her country's government.

The United Nations' top permanent official—and one of its most visible members—is the secretary-general, who has been described as "the eyes, the ears, the mind, the heart, and the voice of humanity." Appointed by the General Assembly, the secretary-general heads the Secretariat and plays a key role in the peacemaking process, either by direct involvement or by appointing special representatives. If the secretary-general determines that an international matter may threaten world peace and security, he brings it to the attention of the Security Council. First, however, he will make every effort to use diplomacy to defuse potentially dangerous situations.

In 1993, the United Nations headquarters in New York became Ambassador Madeleine Albright's new base. However, her home remained in Washington. Since she was a member of the president's cabinet and the National Security Council as well as a U.N. Security Council member and ambassador, she shuttled between New York and Washington two or three times each week. The ambassadorship not only was a challenge for Albright but also marked a pivotal point in her career: she was now a member of the Washington administration.

The only woman on the 15-member U.N. Security Council, Ambassador Albright speaks to reporters following a special council meeting on February 20, 1994. At Albright's left is Russian Ambassador Yuli Vorontso, who called the meeting to address Russia's participation in possible air strikes against Serbs in Bosnia.

Before her confirmation hearing on January 21, 1993, Albright knew she would face some tough questions about the United Nations from the Senate Foreign Relations Committee. So in her opening statement, Albright admitted that while the United Nations was important to America, it also had many problems. "The United Nations remains bogged down by an unwieldy and inefficiently administered staff, overlapping responsibilities, and a financial crisis," she acknowledged. Albright then pledged her full efforts to creating a more efficient and effective organization. However, she also challenged the Senate to commit to these reforms by appropriating funds to pay the United States' debt to the U.N. of more than $1 billion. Many senators had refused to do so because they believed that the organization was rife with mismanagement.

Albright also stressed her intention to strengthen communication between Congress and the U.N. by instituting an open-door policy, inviting the senators to visit the U.N. whenever possible. "I plan to build cooperative relations between our staffs," she said. "I will consider getting your advice and criticism to be an integral part of my job."

Albright was right about the tough questions she faced at her hearing. Yet she answered all of them forthrightly. Even the prickly senator Jesse Helms, who often expressed disdain for the United Nations, respected Albright's straightforward responses to his questions. She won confirmation easily, thereby becoming the first foreign-born woman to be named United States permanent representative to the United Nations.

In her four years at the U.N., Albright had successes, confrontations, and setbacks. One of her accomplishments—which few believed she could achieve—was to get the necessary votes from the U.N. Security Council to send American-led troops into Haiti, where a military *junta* had taken control in 1991. American troops eventually went as peacekeepers, allowing exiled democratic president Jean-Bertrand Aristide to return to power in October 1994. Additionally, Albright was instrumental in creating war-crimes tribunals to bring to justice those responsible for committing atrocities in the former Yugoslav republics and in the African country of Rwanda.

One of Madeleine Albright's most controversial moments came in February 1996, after Cuban pilots shot down two American civilian planes—even though the civilian planes were clearly in international airspace at the time. Infuriated by the incident, Albright pre-

Secretary-General Boutros Boutros-Ghali addresses an audience gathered to commemorate the 50th anniversary of the United Nations as Under Secretary-General Gillian M. Sorensen and Albright look on. Albright later led the campaign to prevent Boutros-Ghali's reelection.

sented the United Nations with a transcript in which one of the Cuban pilots bragged about having had the *cojones* (Spanish for "testicles") to shoot down the planes. Having read the transcript herself, Albright said, she was "struck by the joy of these pilots in committing cold-blooded murder and their use of common vulgarity to describe what they needed to shoot down unarmed civilians. Frankly, this is not *cojones*. This is cowardice." While the remark offended many of the male delegates to the United Nations, President Clinton's reaction to Albright's comment was quite different. He called it "probably the most effective one-liner in the whole administration's foreign policy."

If Madeleine Albright was uncomfortable being one of only four female U.N. ambassadors out of 185 or the only woman on the 15-member U.N. Security Council, she did not show it. Her relaxed demeanor and disarming sense of humor tends to put at ease nearly everyone she meets. Albright was once seen on the assembly floor teaching a fellow diplomat how to dance the macarena. Another time, she left small valentine gifts on the chairs of fellow Security Council members, with notes telling them how proud she was "to sit with 14 handsome young men."

One of Albright's colleagues confirmed her ability to charm: "[She] has the capacity to sit through tedious meetings, to broker differences, to listen to people, to find common ground. In other words, when you're dealing with [so many] different countries, it's the people skills that matter, and she has them."

Believing in the importance of cultivating good relations with her colleagues, Albright also made it a point to visit the homeland of every member of the Security Council and to meet each country's foreign minister. Although this style of diplomacy succeeded with her fellow council members, she ran into difficulty with Secretary-General Boutros Boutros-Ghali of Egypt, who was elected in 1992.

Some time after Albright became ambassador, she began to feel as though Boutros-Ghali was overstepping his bounds. She believed that he was endangering both her position and the reputation of the United States at the U.N. by agreeing with the American position on specific issues and then negotiating alternate solutions without consulting the United States. Initially, the White House was not concerned about this problem, however, since Boutros-Ghali had promised to serve only one term, which would end in 1997. But as the end of his term approached, Boutros-Ghali seemed to have no intention of relinquishing his post.

After several clashes with the secretary-general, Albright became convinced that he was not following the United Nations principle of impartiality, nor was he working to reform the U.N. itself. Rather, he seemed more interested in promoting his own views and agenda. At the same time, the predominantly Republican U.S. Senate, hoping to force reform at the U.N., was still withholding the funds needed to pay off the U.S. debt to the organization. In Albright's eyes, the longer that debt went unpaid, the more the United States would lose credibility with other General Assembly members. It seemed clear that she would not be able to fulfill the goals she set forth in her job as long as Boutros-Ghali remained secretary-general.

At the end of 1996, the United States announced that it would not hesitate to use its U.N. veto power to deny Boutros-Ghali a second term. Many member nations objected to what they felt were strong-arm tactics on the part of the United States. However, the United States had made it clear that its position was nonnegotiable. Boutros-Ghali had to go.

In a final attempt to allow the longtime Egyptian diplomat a graceful exit, the United States offered him the honorary title of secretary-general emeritus. When this overture failed, the United States followed through on its promise to veto the secretary-general's reelection. Though the United States stood alone in its resolve to oust Boutros-Ghali, it was ultimately successful. On December 13, 1996, Kofi Annan of Ghana was unanimously elected the new United Nations secretary-general. Annan has been well received by his U.N. colleagues for his strong advocacy of wholesale organizational reform and his commitment to making the United Nations stronger, leaner, and better managed than ever.

The Boutros-Ghali affair could have been a professional disaster for Madeleine Albright. Instead, it further convinced President Bill Clinton of her capabilities as a skilled foreign-policy diplomat. He knew that the U.N. ambassador would continue to be an invaluable member of his administration. Clinton's reelection in 1996 presented an opportunity for Madeleine Albright to rise to yet another level in her distinguished career.

Secretary of State Albright during a January 1998 news conference on Iraq. "I do not believe that things happen accidentally," Madeleine Albright has said of her appointment to the fourth-highest-ranking government position in America. "I believe you earn them."

9

PLANNING THE FUTURE, DISCOVERING THE PAST

For Madeleine Albright, Bill Clinton's reelection held both personal and professional significance. Not only had he been her boss during his previous term in office but he and his wife, Hillary, were also friends of Albright's. From a professional standpoint, the Democratic victory meant that she would have a job in Clinton's administration for the next four years. In what capacity, however, she was not sure.

Only a few weeks earlier, rumors had been circulating within Washington political circles that the current secretary of state, Warren Christopher, would be stepping down. Christopher confirmed the rumors on November 7th, when he officially announced his retirement during a White House ceremony attended by the president and first lady. Christopher thanked Clinton, who spoke highly of the secretary of state, expressing regret over his resignation and "deep gratitude" for his extraordinary service. The president then announced that he would begin an intensive search for a new secretary of state. Among those being considered were Senate Majority Leader George Mitchell, National Security Advisor Anthony Lake, and U.N. Ambassador Madeleine Albright.

Clinton examined the merits of each candidate, seeking the opinions of others, including his wife and Vice President Al Gore. Though Clinton had no doubts about Albright's qualifications, he was concerned about how a female secretary of state would be received by the leaders of the Arab countries of the Middle East, where women are often viewed as second-class citizens. However, Albright's success in representing the United States in the male-dominated environment of the United Nations ultimately convinced the president that her gender would not affect her ability to handle the post.

Other factors contributed to Clinton's belief that Albright was the best candidate for the position. First, she had proven her ability to articulate Clinton's foreign policy in a way that the average American could follow. In December 1996, *Time* magazine described her as "the master of the sound bite, explaining complex issues in 10-second phrases that lunch-pail Americans can understand." While Clinton was deciding whom to appoint, he kept recalling a conversation with Senator Barbara Mikulski, in which the senator praised Albright for being the only diplomat who could clearly explain to someone like Mikulski's mother, a grocer, why the United States was in Bosnia.

Additionally, having spent four years at the U.N., Albright was familiar with the intricacies of nearly every current international issue. She also had strong bipartisan support from Congress, including the backing of the chairman of the Senate Foreign Relations Committee, Jesse Helms.

Albright has tremendous media and public appeal as well. She is charismatic and outspoken but takes the issues at hand more seriously than she takes herself. For most Americans, she personifies a gung-ho attitude toward the United States as a premier world power. Albright's qualities—her skills, education, personal appeal, and experience—convinced Clinton that she was the best person for the position. And so on Decem-

ber 5, the president presented Albright as his nominee for secretary of state of the United States.

Before she assumed the post, however, she had to be confirmed by the Senate. The confirmation hearing convened January 8, 1997, a historic day on Capitol Hill for a number of reasons. Not only was the committee assembling to interview the first female secretary-of-state-designate, but also, at Albright's request, the outgoing secretary was introducing her. No outgoing secretary of state had ever done so. In his remarks to the committee, Warren Christopher said of Albright:

Albright and President Clinton enjoy a lighthearted moment during a U.N. General Assembly meeting in 1997. Although Clinton denied having named Albright secretary of state simply because she is female, he expressed pride that he had the opportunity to make history by doing so.

> All who know Ambassador Albright admire her keen intellect, her moral strength, and her powerful sense of history, borne of personal experience. . . . Her childhood taught her that freedom can never be taken for granted, and . . . American leadership is always critical to the defense of liberty. Throughout her career, she has applied those lessons to the benefit of the United States and of the world as a whole.

The interior minister of Bahrain meets Albright as she arrives in that country on November 16, 1997. Responding to concerns that she would not fare well in the male-dominated Middle East, Albright has observed that being female is an advantage because "people are intrigued by the fact that I'm a woman, and it helps get the message across."

Despite his negative opinions on the U.N., Jesse Helms was nonetheless a strong proponent of Albright's confirmation. He liked her hawkish manner and anticommunist convictions. In fact, before Clinton announced his cabinet appointees, Helms had sent a memo to the White House identifying who would—and would not—make it past the committee. Albright topped his list of "woulds."

Albright was well acquainted with most of the committee members, having worked on Capitol Hill for more than 25 years. One of those with whom she was most familiar was Christopher Dodd. Albright and Dodd's brother served together on the faculty at Georgetown University, and Dodd himself had been on the committee that, four years earlier, had confirmed Albright's nomination as U.N. ambassador. Now,

Dodd recalled the sacrifices that Josef Korbel made for his family: "I suspect there is great rejoicing in the heavens," Dodd said of Albright's late father, "that 49 years ago a person made a very courageous and difficult decision to leave his own country and adopt this nation. . . . And today [his daughter is] before us as the nominee to be the Secretary of State of this country."

Some observers commented that Albright seemed to breeze through her hearings. Historically, however, such sessions are lengthy and grueling. For Madeleine, it was once again her hard work that made the process look easy. "People say to me, 'Oh, you sailed through your confirmation hearings,'" Albright says. "Well, I studied. My Christmas vacation was a little like college, when everybody went skiing, and I sat and studied."

On January 23, 1997, addressing the press and several distinguished guests, including Madeleine Albright's three daughters, Clinton presented the newly confirmed secretary of state:

> As our U.N. Ambassador these last four years, [Madeleine Albright] has stood unflinchingly for America's interests and values. Now as our Secretary of State, she will help lead the effort to build a world where America makes the most of its partnerships with friends and allies around the world; where America leads the fight for a world that is safer from weapons of terror and mass destruction; where America leads the fight for a world that is safer from organized crime and drug trafficking and all terrorist activity; and where expanded trade brings growth and opportunity; where peace and freedom know no frontiers.

Four days after Albright officially assumed her new post, her deputy secretary, Strobe Talbott, introduced her to her staff at the State Department. Albright discussed her intentions, her priorities, and the way in which she would conduct business in the department. She began by assuring her staff that she was accessible, and she promised that many more meetings, both for-

Sporting her favorite cowboy hat, Secretary Albright disembarks from her state plane in Russia in February 1997.

mal and informal, would take place over the next four years. She was also careful to describe her management style: "Now, I need to tell you and warn you, I'm not exactly hierarchical," she said. "I make phone calls to people that are not directly below me. I reach out— sometimes you may like that, sometimes it might make you nervous. . . . We are all in this together, and I want very much to work with all of you as [much as] I can."

If the State Department staff found Albright's straightforward approach refreshing, they must have delighted in her sense of humor. In the days following her swearing-in, she had frequently been asked how it felt to be the first female secretary of state. She had finally come up with an answer, she told her staff. "[Y]ou may have noticed that I don't exactly look like Secretary Christopher," she said with a smile. "I've never been Secretary of State before, [but] I have been a woman for almost 60 years, so we're now going to see how you put the two together." In closing, Albright told her staff about a conversation she'd had recently with former secretary of state George Shultz, who told her that he believed "the [State] Department is happiest when it is the busiest." She added: "If that is true, we should have a very happy next few years."

Madeleine Albright had reached the pinnacle of her professional career. But throughout her life, as she achieved one success after another, her refugee roots were never far from her thoughts. She often quotes her father in speeches, and she openly shares her family history. However, there was a part of that history that she did not know—and it would be made public shortly after her swearing-in.

The new secretary of state had always been a very vocal proponent of international human rights. While visiting Rwanda as U.N. ambassador in January 1996, for example, she witnessed the human remains from a bloody intertribal war being carefully excavated for proper burial. One skeleton in particular caught her attention because it seemed to have been a child the size of one of her own young grandsons. "You know," she said, after taking a moment to collect herself, "they say in the foreign policy business we aren't supposed to let ourselves be influenced by emotion, but how can we forget that murdered children are not emotions, but that they are human beings whose potential contributions are forever lost."

Albright was a fierce advocate of establishing an international war-crimes tribunal to punish those responsible for atrocities committed in countries like Rwanda and Bosnia. In a speech given at the U.S. Holocaust Memorial Museum in Washington, D.C., in April 1994, she

reiterated America's position on human rights violations: "We oppose amnesty for the architects of ethnic
cleansing," she declared. "We believe that establishing
the truth about what happened in Bosnia is essential
to—not an obstacle to—nations' reconciliation."

Shortly after Madeleine Albright assumed her new
position as secretary of state, a story about her family
appeared in the *Washington Post*. The article, written by
Michael Dobbs, revealed that although Albright had
been raised as a Catholic (she became Episcopalian when
she married), her family was actually of Jewish descent.
Dobbs cited Czech documents, Nazi records published
by a Holocaust research center, and Auschwitz transport
lists that identified several members of Albright's family
as having died in the Terezin and Auschwitz concentration camps, including Josef Korbel's parents and her
cousin Dagmar Simova's mother, father, and sister.

Albright's initial reaction to the story was to say that
she found the information "compelling" but wished to
examine it further herself. She felt that the matter was
personal and not one she wished to discuss with the
press in detail. Nevertheless, other newspapers and
magazines quickly picked up the story and asked
Albright to address the revelations about her family.

Some weeks after the *Post* article appeared, and after
Albright felt that she had come to terms with the part
of her past she had just learned about, she granted an
exclusive interview to Lally Weymouth of *Newsweek*
magazine. First and foremost in the *Newsweek* interview, Albright wanted to set the record straight about
the facts surrounding the story of her Jewish roots. She
told Weymouth that despite reports to the contrary, she
had never said that she was surprised to learn of her
true origins. What did surprise her, she said, was learning that her grandparents and other family members
had died in Nazi concentration camps.

Albright defended the decision her parents made not
to tell their children about their conversion or about

the way her grandparents died. "What they gave us children was the gift of life, literally," she said of Josef and Mandula. "Twice, once by giving us birth and the other by bringing us to America to escape what, clearly now, would have been certain death. So I am not going to question their motives." She concluded the interview by saying, "I have been proud of the heritage that I have known about and I will be equally proud of the heritage that I have just been given."

Not long after the *Washington Post* article was published, Albright's brother, John Korbel, and sister, Kathy Silva, went to Prague to review the documents Dobbs had cited in his article. They also visited the city's Pinkas Synagogue, where the names of 77,297 Czech Holocaust victims are recorded on the walls. The experience was very emotional for Albright's siblings. "When we went to the wall and saw those names it was just undoing," Kathy recalled. She said to her brother, "John, do you realize if [our parents] had not done what they did, their names and Madeleine's would be up here and we wouldn't be looking at it?"

Madeleine Albright understands that line of thinking all too well: "I somehow felt that I had been saved—I thought only from the Russians—in order to repay that debt, to repay the fact that I was a free person. I guess it's truer than ever now."

In mid-July 1997, Albright returned to her homeland for the first time in her capacity as secretary of state. Though she was there on an official visit to meet with Czech president Václav Havel, Albright also had a personal reason for her visit. Immediately after arriving in the Czech Republic, she went to the Pinkas Synagogue and entered it alone, without the usual entourage of reporters. There, on a side wall near the front of the synagogue, Albright found what she had gone inside to see—the names of her grandparents, Arnost and Olga Korbel. She was also taken to Prague's Jewish Town Hall, where she viewed the documents

(continued on page 120)

In a bitter reminder of the atrocities of the Holocaust, a 1945 photograph depicting emaciated Buchenwald concentration camp prisoners (facing page) is reproduced on the wall of Yad Vashem, Jerusalem's Holocaust memorial and museum, which Madeleine Albright visited in September 1997. The face of Nobel Peace Prize–winner and author Elie Wiesel can be seen on the far right in the second cubicle from the left, third bunk from the top, in the original photograph.

Secretary of State Madeleine K. Albright's Remarks at the Jewish Museum in Prague, Czech Republic, July 13, 1997

I have visited the Old Jewish Cemetery in Prague a number of times before. I have always been struck by its serene beauty and its importance as a symbol of the richness and the antiquity of Jewish life here.

For a long time, the Pinkas Synagogue was closed. The first time I went into the Synagogue was one year ago along with the First Lady, Mrs. Hillary Rodham Clinton. At that time, I was deeply moved by the thousands of names carved on the wall. But because I did not know my own family story then, it didn't occur to me to look for the names of my grandparents or other family members.

Tonight, I knew to look for those names—and their image will forever be seared into my heart. Many have written about the horror of the Holocaust, and I have grown up thinking about it, speaking about it, and trying to incorporate its lessons into my work. Now that I am aware of my own Jewish background—and the fact that my grandparents died in concentration camps—the evil of the Holocaust has an even more personal meaning for me, and I feel an even greater determination to ensure that it will never be forgotten.

As I stood looking at that melancholy wall, all the walls, I not only grieved for those members of my family whose names were inscribed there, but I also thought about my parents. I thought about the choice they made. They clearly confronted the most excruciating decision a human being can face when they left members of their family behind even as they saved me from certain death. I will always love and honor my parents and will always respect their decision, for that most painful of choices gave me life a second time.

Identity is a complex compilation of influences and experiences—past and present. I have always felt that my life has been strengthened and enriched by my heritage and my past. And I have always felt that my life story is also the story of the evil of totalitarianism and the turbulence of 20th century Europe. To the many values and many facets that make up who I am, I now add the knowledge that my grandparents and members of my family perished in the worst catastrophe in human history.

So I leave here tonight with the certainty that this new part of my identity adds something stronger, sadder, and richer to my life.

On a private one-day visit to the Czech Republic in September 1997, a tearful Madeleine Albright listens as a resident of her mother's hometown recounts his memories of Josef and Mandula Korbel.

(continued from page 117)

that confirmed that her grandparents had died in two different concentration camps. Filled with emotion, Albright later expressed an even stronger determination to ensure that the horror of the Holocaust would never be forgotten.

Over the next few days, Albright met with President Havel and other Czech leaders to discuss the country's pending acceptance into the North Atlantic Treaty Organization (NATO) along with Hungary and Poland, former members of the Soviet bloc. She also had breakfast with her cousin Dagmar. Later, in an address to the Czech people, Albright identified three significant journeys which had brought her to this moment:

> I have been thinking about the memories and the meaning of my own family's journey through the war and the turbulence of postwar Europe to the freedom and security of the United States. I have been thinking as well about Europe's journey from total war to absolute division to the promise of enduring unity and peace. And of course, I have been thinking about the journey of the Czech nation from the day in 1918 when its independence was proclaimed on this very spot, to the day in 1948 when its liberty was extinguished, to this day, when you take your rightful place in the family of European democracies—fully, finally and forever.

Though the confirming evidence of the suffering and death of family members was terribly painful for Albright, the trip "home" had its joyous moments too. She was filled with pride upon meeting President Václav Havel, her friend and the leader of what was now a free and democratic nation, the country that had been her parents' passion. No doubt Josef and Mandula Korbel would have been proud to see their eldest daughter, who represents the most powerful democratic country in the world, speaking about a brighter, more promising future for the people of the Czech Republic.

Before Albright's visit to the Czech Republic ended, President Havel bestowed upon her the medal of the Order of the White Lion, the country's highest decoration, during a ceremony at Hradčany Castle. Later, while strolling through a part of Prague's historic area, Albright came upon a group of American tourists. One family told her that they were from Denver. "Ah, my second home town," replied Albright, the world traveler.

In her first year as secretary of state, Madeleine Albright traveled ceaselessly, visiting 12 states in the United States and many countries in Europe, the Mid-

Czech president Václav Havel awards Secretary of State Madeleine Albright with the Order of the White Lion, the highest honor of the Czech Republic, on July 14, 1997. Recalling her first meeting with Havel in 1989, the daughter of a Czech diplomat said, "There was this instant when I thought, I've spent my whole life preparing, I've learned all these things so . . . I could advise the Czech president."

dle East, Asia, and Africa. Her cordial but firm style of diplomacy has required some adjustments from her foreign counterparts. However, she has moved unflinchingly through the male-dominated world of foreign relations. Using her unique mix of tough talk and charm, she has effectively communicated America's policies while earning the respect of her colleagues at home and abroad.

Though Albright has made it clear that she will not be bullied or intimidated, she also demonstrates her willingness to play on her own femininity to make her point or win a new ally. She delighted Jesse Helms, whom she had first charmed during the confirmation hearing for her U.N. ambassador position, by presenting the senator with a T-shirt that reads, "Somebody at the State Department Loves Me." During one of her meetings with Russian foreign minister Yevgeni Primakov, Albright gave him an autographed picture of President Clinton for his granddaughter.

But Albright is quick to detect condescension: when she presented Serbian leader Slobodan Milosevic with a long list of his peace accord violations, he cut her off by saying with a patronizing smile, "Madame Secretary, you're not well informed." His attempt to rattle Albright backfired. "Don't tell me I'm uninformed," she snapped. "I lived here." Milosevic's smile vanished.

On January 13, 1998, Albright made her first speech of the year, not only outlining the United States's foreign policy agenda for 1998 but also reviewing her achievements—as well as her unfinished business—during her first year as secretary of state. Describing 1997 as "extraordinary," she shared some of her personal highlights, including throwing the first baseball for the Baltimore Orioles on opening day and being listed in *Time* magazine as one of the most influential people of the year.

On the diplomatic front, after much effort and with bipartisan support, Albright succeeded in having the United States named one of the original members of the Chemical Weapons Convention, an organization dedicated to opposing the spread of weapons of mass destruction. She had lobbied hard for America to take a lead role in this matter.

The United States also signed new defense guidelines with Japan, and continued dialogue with Communist China regarding security and human rights produced some progress, including the release of Chinese dissident Wei Jingsheng.

And although the Middle East continues to be a trouble spot, Albright remains determined to help create a lasting peace in that region. She has stressed that the United States is firm in its resolve to see Iraqi

An unlikely pair: wearing his gift T-shirt from Albright, Senator Jesse Helms confers with the secretary of state during an inter-staff softball game. "I don't always agree with her," Helms says of Albright, "but she is not p.c. She is just honest; that goes a long way with me."

leader Saddam Hussein comply with all U.N. Security Council resolutions, including unconditional access for United Nations Special Commission (UNSCOM) inspectors to suspected Iraqi weapons sites. Using the Iraq standoff as an example, Albright has once again urged Congress to pay off its debt to the United Nations, repeating her belief that the effectiveness of the U.N. depends on the financial as well as diplomatic support of its members.

One might imagine that being secretary of state for a world power would be an exhausting and difficult job. That may be true, but Madeleine Albright claims to love what she does. "[M]y friends tell me it shows on my face," she said in an interview for the CBS special *Ladies Home Journal's Ten Most Fascinating Women of 1997.* "I get up with great pleasure every morning, except when I think I have to exercise," she added drolly. But she also emphasized that she could not have attained this post on her own: "I know that I would not be in this job were it not for incredible support from a lot of people, men and women. And I want to make sure that as I do this job, I always remember how I got here and why I'm here."

The world is a very different place today than it was when Marie Jana Korbel was born. It has changed greatly since Madeleine and her family came to America in 1948. Communism is no longer a threat in Europe. Great strides have been made in the efforts to establish and maintain worldwide peace and to monitor and prevent human rights violations around the globe. Albright herself is proof that opportunities for women have expanded in fields that were once the exclusive domain of men. "Madeleine Albright," said President Clinton, "embodies the best of America. It says something about our country . . . that a young girl raised in the shadow of Nazi aggression in Czechoslovakia can rise to the highest diplomatic office in America."

Through hard work, determination, and perseverance,

Albright has achieved what no other woman has. She continues to work tirelessly for peace and human rights worldwide, voicing the democratic principles on which her adoptive homeland was founded. Albright truly is a role model for people of all ages in all professions. She is a source of great pride to those whom she has followed and an inspiration to succeeding generations.

Never forgetting her own past, the secretary of state addressed a group of refugee children in Sarajevo in June 1997. "Everything will be okay," she told them, "because we will make the world good for you."

CHRONOLOGY

1937 Marie (Madeleine) Jana Korbel born in Prague, Czechoslovakia, to Josef and Mandula Korbel

1939 Germany invades Czechoslovakia; the Korbels flee to England

1942 Sister, Katharine, is born

1945 World War II ends; the Korbels return to Czechoslovakia

1947 Madeleine attends boarding school in Switzerland; brother, John, is born

1948 After a political coup in Czechoslovakia, Mandula Korbel and her children flee to the United States; Josef later joins them, seeking political asylum

1949 The Korbels move from New York to Colorado, where Josef accepts a position at the University of Denver

1955 Graduates from Kent School for Girls

1959 Graduates from Wellesley College; marries Joseph Medill Patterson Albright

1961 Twins Anne and Alice are born

1967 Daughter Katharine is born

1968 Earns master's degree; moves to Washington, D.C.

1976 Earns Ph.D.; becomes chief legislative assistant to Senator Edmund M. Muskie

1977 Father, Josef Korbel, dies

1978 Becomes aide to National Security Council advisor Zbigniew Brzezinski

1982 Joins faculty of Georgetown University School of Foreign Service as research professor of international affairs, where she serves for 11 years; is divorced from Joseph Medill Patterson Albright

1989 Mother, Mandula Korbel, dies

1993 Appointed U.S. permanent representative to the United Nations

1995 Receives Award of Honor from the New York Association for New Americans

1996 Receives Sara Lee Corporation Frontrunner Award

1997 Appointed 64th secretary of state of the United States, the first woman to hold the position

1999 Supports role of U.S. troops in Kosovo; her central and vocal role in the injustice leads to the nickname "Madeleine's War"

Albright, Anne. "Your Mom's on the Floor with the Senator, Kids." *Newsweek*, 10 February 1997.

Bartz, Carl F. *The Department of State*. New York: Chelsea House, 1989.

Baum, Geraldine. "A Diplomatic Core: Madeleine Albright is the First Line of Defense for U.S. Foreign Policy." *Los Angeles Times*, 8 February 1995.

Blood, Thomas. *Madam Secretary: A Biography of Madeleine Albright*. New York: St. Martin's Press, 1997.

Crossette, Barbara. "A Political Diplomat: Madeleine Korbel Albright." *New York Times*, 6 December 1996.

Culver, Virginia. "Albright Scopes Summit Sites." *Denver Post*, 14 May 1997.

Dobbs, Michael. "Out of the Past." *Washington Post*, 9 February 1997.

_____. "West Making Amends, Albright Tells Czechs." *Washington Post*, 15 July 1997.

Dobbs, Michael, and John Goshko. "Albright's Personal Odyssey Shaped Foreign Policy Beliefs." *Washington Post*, 6 December 1996.

Fedarko, Kevin. "Clinton's Blunt Instrument." *Time*, 31 October 1994.

Gibbs, Nancy. "Voice of America." *Time*, 16 December 1996.

_____. "The Many Lives of Madeleine." *Time*, 17 February 1997.

Lewis, Gavin. *Tomáš Masaryk*. New York: Chelsea House, 1990.

Maas, Robert. *U.N. Ambassador: A Behind-the-Scenes Look at Madeleine Albright*. New York: Walker & Company, 1995.

Parker, Nancy Winslow. *The President's Cabinet and How It Grew*. New York: Harper Collins, 1991.

Pollard, Michael. *United Nations*. New York: MacMillan Publishing Company, 1993.

Reed, Julia. "Woman of the World." *Vogue*, September 1997.

Sinclair, Molly. "Woman on Top of the World." *Washington Post*, 6 January 1991.

Waller, Douglas. "The Albright Touch." *Time*, 16 June 1997.

Weymouth, Lally. "As I Find Out More, I'm Very Proud." *Newsweek*, 24 February 1997.

Wepman, Dennis. *Adolf Hitler*. New York: Chelsea House, 1985.

APPENDIX

FIND OUT MORE ABOUT THE U.S. DEPARTMENT OF STATE

Address and Phone:

2201 C Street, N.W.
Washington, DC 20520
202-647-4000
publicaffairs@panet.us-state.gov
secretary@state.gov

Websites:

http://www.state.gov/index.html (State Dept. home page)

http://secretary.state.gov/index.html (Madeleine Albright's home
   page)

http://www.state.gov/www/regions_digital.html (special site for
   students)

FIND OUT MORE ABOUT THE UNITED NATIONS

Address and Phone:

Public Inquiries Unit
United Nations
Room GA-57
New York, NY 10017
212-963-4475

Websites:

http://www.un.org (main page)

http://www.un.org/Pubs/CyberSchoolBus (special site for kids)

http://www.unausa.org (United Nations Association home page)

THE MODEL UNITED NATIONS (MUN):

The MUN provides simulations of United Nations activities for
high school and college students worldwide. Using accurate
information about current international situations, students assume
the roles of nations' delegates in simulated sessions of the General
Assembly, the Security Council, and various U.N. committees.

For information on the MUN in the United States, contact:

New York Headquarters
United Nations Association-USA
801 Second Avenue
New York, NY 10017
212-907-1300
unahq@unausa.org

Washington Office
1779 Massachusetts Avenue, N.W.
Suite 610
Washington, DC 20036
202-462-3446
unadc@unausa.org

INDEX

INDEX

PICTURE CREDITS

The author wishes to thank Susan E. Walitsky, Director of Media Outreach, U.S. Department of State, for her assistance in securing many of the photographs of Secretary of State Albright and her family.

Judy L. Hasday, a native of Philadelphia, Pennsylvania, received a B.A. in communications and an Ed.M. in instructional technologies from Temple University. A multimedia professional, she has had her photographs published in several magazines and books, including a number of Chelsea House titles. She is also a freelance author of biographies for young adults, including *James Earl Jones.*

Matina S. Horner was president of Radcliffe College and associate professor of psychology and social relations at Harvard University. She is best known for her studies of women's motivation, achievement, and personality development. Dr. Horner has served on several national boards and advisory councils, including those of the National Science Foundation, Time Inc., and the Women's Research and Education Institute. She earned her B.A. from Bryn Mawr College and her Ph.D. from the University of Michigan, and holds honorary degrees from many colleges and universities, including Mount Holyoke, Smith, Tufts, and the University of Pennsylvania.